The Kingdom of Swaziland

Robert H. Davies
Dan O'Meara
Sipho Dlamini

The Kingdom of Swaziland

— A Profile

Robert H. Davies
Dan O'Meara
Sipho Dlamini

Zed Books Ltd.

The Kingdom of Swaziland was first published by Zed Books
Ltd., 57 Caledonian Road, London N1 9BU, in 1985.

Copyright © Robert H. Davies, Dan O'Meara,
Sipho Dlamini, 1985.

Cover designed by Lee Robinson.
Printed by The Bath Press, Avon.

British Library Cataloguing in Publication Data
Davies, Robert H.
    The Kingdom of Swaziland : a profile.
    1. Swaziland — Social conditions
    I. Title   II. O'Meara, Dan   III. Dlamini, Sipho
    968.1'303   HN805.A8

    ISBN 0-86232-449-1
    ISBN 0-86232-450-5 Pbk

US Distributor
Biblio Distribution Center, 81 Adams Drive,
Totowa, New Jersey 07512

Contents

Tables

Acknowledgement

This book could not have been written without the extensive and generous cooperation of the former Dean of the Arts Faculty and former Director of the Social Science Research Unit at the University of Swaziland, Professor John Daniel. This analysis will remain a 'profile' on Swaziland until John Daniel's own research work is published – hopefully in the near future.

Introduction

The Kingdom of Swaziland is a small, landlocked enclave in south-eastern Africa, completely surrounded by the Republic of South Africa to the north, west and south, and the Peoples Republic of Mozambique to the east. It covers an area of just 17,364 square kilometres, making it, after the Gambia, the smallest country in continental Africa. Its population in 1980 was 547,452. Of all the countries on the African continent, only Djibouti has a smaller population. In 1981 the GNP per capita was estimated to have reached $800, elevating Swaziland out of the ranks of the world's 25 poorest countries.

Swaziland gained its independence from Britain in 1968 under a constitutional monarchy. However, since the 'King's coup' in 1973, the country has been ruled by a conservative alliance organized through the Swazi monarchy. All forms of opposition to the prevailing form of state, and its very close connections with the apartheid regime in South Africa, have been vigorously suppressed. Following the death of King Sobhuza II in August 1982, an intense power struggle has developed within the ruling groups, resulting in a series of political crises and an intensification of political repression. Swaziland is currently regarded as fairly unstable.

The country is a member of two regional organizations. In the Southern African Customs Union it is grouped with South Africa, Lesotho and Botswana – and, in effect, also with the South African colony of Namibia. Its membership of the Southern African Development Coordination Conference formally aligns Swaziland with eight states of the region in a common effort to reduce their economic dependence on South Africa.

This Profile is intended as a general background study of this southern African state. It deals with the following themes: Swaziland under colonialism; the process of decolonization; the structure of the Swazi economy since independence; the class structure of Swaziland; political struggles since independence; Swaziland in the southern African region.

1. Swaziland Under Colonialism

Swaziland is often grouped together with Botswana and Lesotho as one of the so-called BLS countries. This reflects the fact that under colonialism all three territories were administered as British Protectorates by the same British High Commissioner based in Pretoria, and were often referred to collectively as the 'High Commission territories'. However, when considering patterns of accumulation and class structure, such a joint classification is less useful. Although each country was subordinated as a labour reservoir for South African capitalism, in the case of Swaziland – as distinct from that of Lesotho and Botswana – there also emerged a significant locally based capitalist sector. For this reason a number of recent analyses argue that in important respects the colonial heritage of Swaziland has more in common with that of Zimbabwe. One indication of the importance of locally based capitalist production was that the country was a relatively modest supplier of labour to the South African mining industry. It never furnished more than 4% of the mine labour force, and frequently much less.

The Kingdom of Swaziland came into being in the violent upheavals – known as the *Mfecane* – which transformed African societies in southern Africa in the first 25 years of the 19th Century. The Dlamini clan consolidated its dominance over an area larger than present day Swaziland, extracting surplus in the form of tribute from the population of the region. The Swazi kings strove, through a shifting web of alliances, to protect their independence from the powerful Zulu kingdom

1

to the south, and, after 1852, from the Boer republic of the Transvaal to the west.[1]

Swaziland was formally declared a British Protectorate in 1881. The British sought to prevent the incorporation of the kingdom either by the Transvaal Boer republic, or by the Portuguese colony of Mozambique, both of whose rulers had laid claim to Swaziland. Thereafter large numbers of prospectors, land speculators and Boer farmers seeking winter grazing lands, bribed, cajoled and otherwise persuaded the then Swazi king Mbadzeni to cede to them large parts of the kingdom. In this wave of concessions, Mbadzeni in many cases granted rights over the same areas to several claimants. The resulting confusion provided the British colonial authorities with an opportunity to intervene. The reports of three commissions of enquiry into concessions between 1904 and 1908 set the pattern for the future. These recommended that two thirds of the kingdom (including all the best grazing land and the known mineral areas) be conceded to foreign concessionaries. The remaining third would be 'reserved' for the 'Swazi nation', and was later known as 'Swazi Nation Land'.

These recommendations were eventually implemented in 1914, one year after a similar measure in South Africa – the 1913 Natives Land Act – reserved a mere 8% of that country for Africans and severely restricted African occupation of rural land. A wave of forced removals pushed Swazis occupying land outside the designated Swazi Nation areas back into these reserves. This was followed in 1915 by the introduction of hut taxes to force Swazi peasants to make themselves available as wage labourers for both settler capitalists and the South African mining industry.

Capitalist production emerged in Swaziland through these processes of primitive accumulation. Prior to the Second World War there existed two principal forms of capitalist production:

a) **mining**. This was dominated by British capital. Initially the principal minerals mined were gold and tin, but the returns proved disappointing. However, in the 1930s large deposits of asbestos were discovered in the north-west region of the country. In 1938 the British multinational Turner & Newell opened up the profitable Havelock asbestos mine which is still in operation.

b) **settler-farming**. This was primarily orientated around cattle ranching in the early colonial period, while tobacco and cotton farming later also emerged. The early development of this sector grew largely out of the actions of a number of land speculators who sold farming land to settler farmers. The leading land speculator, Alistair Miller, has been described as 'a scaled-down version of Cecil Rhodes . . . a visionary and a man of boundless energy . . . a cunning schemer and a thorough-going bigot'.[2] Through his 'mushroom land settlement scheme' Miller sought to settle expropriated Swazi lands with 'good British stock', keeping Afrikaners out of the colony. However, a number of British settlers recruited under these schemes eventually sold up to Afrikaner farmers, many of whom used their Swazi properties only as winter grazing land.

Between the Second World War and independence in 1968, new forms of production were developed. Both British and South African capitalists made significant new investments in mining ventures. The Anglo American Corporation opened up Swaziland's largest coal mine at Mpaka – which it continues to operate. Anglo was also the major shareholder in the South African-British consortium which established the Ngwenya iron ore mine. This operated from 1964 to 1977. Virtually all of the output was exported to Japan via a railway specially built for the purpose, connecting the mine to the port of Maputo (then known as Lourenço Marques).

This period also saw the development of a plantation sector, controlled by British multinationals. Among the most important of the new ventures were:

i) irrigated sugar planations – through the Commonwealth Development Corporation (CDC), a profit-making British parastatal;

ii) forestry and timber – through the CDC in partnership with the British multinational, Courtaulds;
iii) large-scale cattle ranching, in which the Lonrho group was predominant.

Thus, by the end of the colonial period, foreign multinational capital had come to control a substantial part of Swaziland's colonial capitalist economy. The remainder was in the hands of a significant and well-organized settler bourgeoisie, which had its own particular interests to defend.

Throughout the entire colonial period, Swazis were allowed to occupy land only in the so-called Swazi Nation areas – initially designated as one third of the land area of the country. Unable to support themselves in these overcrowded, over-worked areas through family agricultural production alone, the majority of Swazi households were compelled to send at least some of their members to seek wage labour either in South Africa or in the capitalist sectors of Swaziland. How-ever, despite the overall poverty of the Swazi Nation areas, relations between Swazis were not those of equality. Important class differences existed. The dominant class force was the royal family and the chiefs. Under the system of 'indirect rule' instituted by British colonialism, the chiefs and the royal family played a limited administrative role in the Swazi Nation areas. They allocated land and carried out certain administra-tive functions for the colonial authorities; for example, prior to the accession to the Swazi throne of King Sobhuza II in 1922, the Queen Regent played an important role in recruiting labour for the South African mines. The chiefs also extracted a surplus in the form of tribute from their 'subjects'. However due to the restrictions imposed by colonial rule, they had little opportunity to use such exploitation as a base for capitalist accumulation. The largest part of such surplus was in fact used, particularly after the accession of Sobhuza to the throne, to buy back lands alienated by the settlers. Through the cam-paign to 'buy back' Swazi lands, the total area of Swazi Nation Land was in fact extended from one third of the country in 1914 to 45% by independence in 1968.

This 'buy back' campaign won a certain measure of popular support for the king. This was further consolidated as a result of British attitudes to the Swazi monarchy. Under the indirect rule instituted by British colonialism, while the chiefs were given a certain administrative role and status in the colonial system, the monarch himself was to some extent by-passed. The British did not recognize the Swazi monarch as a King (which in tradition he was), but termed him instead Paramount Chief. This meant that the struggle of the monarch to assert his real status as a King had certain anti-colonial overtones; it could be represented as a struggle for the legitimacy of national institutions against colonialism. Coupled with the prestige the King gained from the 'buy back' campaign, this assertion of his status against British belittlement certainly won some popular support and was an important factor in consolidating the political position of the King among the masses in the Swazi Nation areas. As a result, an ideology of traditionalism also gained hold in these areas. All of this was to have important results in the political struggles within Swaziland in the 1960s.

2. The Process of Decolonization

Swaziland's independence in 1968 was not fundamentally the result of pressures from the relatively modest internal anti-colonial struggles. Rather, it stemmed from the strategic decision of the major colonial powers, confronted with intense anti-colonial struggles elsewhere, to abandon formal control over all their African colonies. However the *form* of decolonization in Swaziland was profoundly affected by domestic struggles. By far the most important of these were a series of strikes which began in the timber industry and spread to other sectors in 1962–3. These strikes were mostly in pursuit of demands for higher wages and were accompanied by the formation of a number of trades unions. They represented the most militant phase of working-class struggle in Swaziland's history, and led the colonial regime to call in a battalion of the British army from Kenya to restore 'law and order'.

These strikes imprinted themselves on the decolonization process. Each of the contending political forces was compelled to respond and define its position on industrial relations. This critically affected the line-up of the powerful settler and multi-national bourgeois forces, whose influence on the eventual form of decolonization was substantial.

Four political parties emerged to contest the pre-independence elections of 1964 and 1967. These were: the Imbokodvo National Movement (INM); the Swaziland Democratic Party (SDP); the Swaziland Peoples Party (SPP); and the Ngwane National Liberatory Congress (NNLC).

The INM was formed by King Sobhuza II and was based on

the network of chiefs linked to the royal family which had exercised limited administrative power under colonialism in the Swazi Nation areas. It also proved to have considerable mass support in these areas, which is explained by the ideology of 'traditionalism', and the fact that the King was seen to be personally uncorrupt and fighting to regain the heritage of the Swazi people through the 'buy back' campaign. Sobhuza himself had been reluctant to form a political party, arguing that these were not traditional Swazi institutions and that a party political contest would diminish the stature of the monarchy. Sobhuza would have preferred a system based directly on the *Tinkundla* – local administrative structures controlled by councillors appointed by the King, known as *indunas*. With the emergence of other parties, however, the King was eventually persuaded by van Wyk de Vries, a South African advocate and member of the secret *Afrikaner Broederbond*, that he would need some direct base among the elected members of parliament to secure his position. The King's party favoured a form of state in which the 'traditional' Swazi power structures would have a central place. The party took a strong stand against strikes and was generally critical of trades unions, favouring a system of industrial relations in which disputes would be settled by *indunas* and works councils.[3]

The SDP was formed by Allen and Sishayi Nxumalo. It was based on the small stratum of Swazi professionals who, although linked to the Swazi chieftainship, were not part of the royalist inner circles. The party was strongly pro-capitalist, and favoured a form of state in which the King would play a largely ceremonial role.

The SPP and NNLC grew out of radicalized sections of the petty bourgeoisie. Of the two, the NNLC, formed out of a split in the SPP and led by Dr Ambrose Zwane, was the larger and more important. The NNLC's programme was one of militant, populist pan-Africanism. The party sought to build a mass base, particularly among the working class. It gained considerable support from workers engaged in the 1962–3 strikes, and many trade unionists were NNLC members. However, the NNLC had little support in the Swazi Nation areas.

7

In addition to these parties a number of political associations also emerged from the settler population of almost 10,000. The largest of these, the United Swaziland Association (USA), initially opposed the very notion of independence. However, as political reality pressed on it, it shifted to a position which sought independence on a power sharing basis, with a 50/50 European/African division of parliamentary seats. The INM initially accepted this scheme, and the USA and INM fought the 1964 elections in agreement. However, the INM's across-the-board victory in these elections, and criticism from the opposition parties of a sell out, led the King's party to reverse its earlier position and now advocate a universal franchise without reserved settler representation. This did not lead to a split with the USA however, which, influenced by the so-called Committee of 12 (the larger settler capitalists), came to regard the INM as its best available option. The alliance between the settlers and Swazi royalists was firmly cemented by the time of the 1967 pre-independence elections, when most settlers supported the INM.

Foreign multinational capital was initially less enthusiastic about the INM and the traditional Swazi rulers. Indeed there are indications that significant elements of this class force at first favoured the SDP as a party which they saw bringing a 'modernizing elite' to power. This attitude changed as a result of the role the King played in breaking the 1962–3 strikes. The King's denunciation of the strikers was a major factor isolating them from the masses in the Swazi Nation areas. This experience influenced the major strategists of multinational capital in Swaziland to conclude that a form of state in which the King had a central role would, after all, be the best guarantee of the general social conditions of accumulation. This position was reinforced when the allegiance to the King of the mass of rural voters was demonstrated in the 1964 election, where the INM won 85% of the vote, to 12% for the NNLC. Shortly after the 1964 elections the SDP dissolved itself and its leaders joined the INM.[4]

By the time of the 1967 elections the INM had the firm support of both the settler and the multinational factions of the colonial bourgeoisie. With this backing and its mass base in the rural areas, the party won all parliamentary seats in this election, although the NNLC won 20% of the vote.

Thus Swaziland gained its independence in 1968 as a constitutional monarchy. In terms of the independence constitution Swaziland was governed by a Prime Minister and Cabinet drawn from an elected parliament. Given the INM's monopoly of parliament, the King himself selected the Prime Minister and Cabinet. These were 'traditionally'-oriented. In terms of this constitution, the King was head of state with certain limited executive powers. In practice, however, Sobhuza ruled Swaziland through his Cabinet and parliament. This form of government continued until the political crisis following the 1973 elections (see Chapter 5).

3. The Structure of the Swazi Economy Since Independence

Swaziland's capitalist economy has continued to be thoroughly dominated by foreign monopoly capital since independence in 1968. The government operates an open door policy designed to attract foreign investment to the kingdom. This policy has four major aspects:

● generous incentives, particularly in the form of tax rebates. The rate of company taxation in Swaziland is lower than in South Africa;
● avoidance of nationalization. State policy of 'participation with outside capital' stressed that investors should have a minimum 51% control, and usually an even greater share of locally based undertakings. Minority shareholdings are reserved for two Swazi parastatals (see page 17).
● the free transfer of profits and dividends derived from local trading, subject only to a 15% non-resident shareholder's tax. Interest, royalties and directors' fees are likewise easily transferred out of the country.
● a guaranteed cheap and docile labour force. As a government advertising brochure entitled *Guide for Investors* put it: 'Wages are low in Swaziland even when compared with those in other African countries . . . Swaziland has only one effective trade union . . . strikes are rare.' Government policy is designed to maintain this situation.

Under these conditions substantial foreign investment has flowed into every sector of the economy, with the important

10

exception of mining, where the closure of iron ore operations in 1977 has led to an actual decline. The biggest recipient of this inflow has been the agricultural sector, and in particular the sugar industry. Elsewhere, these policies have stimulated a growth in manufacturing for import substitution concerns, while a flourishing tourist industry has grown up, mainly around the casinos established since independence.

The various sectors of the Swazi economy are analysed below (pages 21–29). Three important changes since 1968 should be noted.

1. Domination by South African Capital

Before independence, South African and British capital separately dominated specific sectors of the Swazi economy and were jointly involved in others. Today, however, British capital is clearly dominant only in the banking sector, through the Standard and Barclays banking groups. The Swazi government has a 40% share of these banks. British dominance of the agricultural sector – i.e. large-scale capitalist agriculture, dominated by the CDC and Lonrho groups – is now being challenged by South African monopolies. Thus the Anglo American Corporation controls 90% of citrus production in Swaziland, while another South African concern, Zululand Food Producers, has recently bought out the British/Swiss company, Libby's, which produces and cans most of Swaziland's pineapples.[5] However, the sugar plantations, which provide the largest single source of export earnings, and, until 1981, the largest single source of government revenue, as well as other large-scale agricultural production, are still largely in the hands of British capital.

The growth in other sectors of the economy has been fuelled largely by South African, or South African-based, investments. In the manufacturing and commercial sectors, the most active investor has been the emerging South African conglomerate, Kirsch Industries.[6] This group dominates maize milling and maize importation. It holds the profitable Mercedes-Benz and Nissan franchises in Swaziland, operates the country's largest trade wholesaler and hardware and agri-

11

cultural stores, and owns 50% of the two largest shopping plazas together with a number of other manufacturing and commercial interests. Other important South African conglomerates maintain manufacturing subsidiaries in Swaziland. Thus the Neopack subsidiary of the Barlow Rand Group dominates the packaging industry, while the Swazi Breweries subsidiary of South African Breweries has a total monopoly of local malt beer production. Most manufacturing industry in Swaziland is in fact controlled by South African companies.

Large-scale commerce is similarly dominated by South African capital. Apart from the interests of the Kirsch group cited above, the country's largest supermarket is a branch of the OK Bazaars subsidiary of South African Breweries, whilst numerous other smaller South African commercial undertakings operate in Swaziland. Moreover, more than 95% of the imports into the kingdom come from South Africa. Thus, with the exception of the few import substitution commodities produced in Swaziland (mainly by South African companies), Swazi commerce consists largely of South African-owned companies selling South African-made products.

The tourist industry is also dominated by South African-based companies. Most important of these is the Sun International group which owns four hotels in Swaziland, including the extremely lucrative Royal Swazi Sun and Nhlangano Sun casinos. Started in 1969, these operations have provided white South Africans with a range of gambling and sexual services banned in South Africa itself, and have inspired their reproduction in other neighbouring states and the 'independent' bantustans. These casinos are probably the most profitable of all foreign investments in Swaziland.

The domination of the Swazi economy by South African capital is in some respects institutionalized through the Southern African Customs Union (SACU). Dating back to 1910, SACU has established a free trade area between the four member countries, the BLS states – Botswana, Lesotho and Swaziland – and South Africa itself. Under this arrangement the BLS countries receive a percentage of the overall customs revenue generated in the region. Between 1910 and

1969 the joint BLS share of the revenue was 1.3109% of the total. South Africa took the rest. This revenue was then divided between the BLS countries by the British colonial administration.

In the colonial period this arrangement gave South African capital free access to the markets of the BLS countries, as well as the raw materials produced in them. In theory the agreement was supposed to provide reciprocal access to the South African market by producers in the BLS countries. Yet in practice BLS commodities which competed with South African products were excluded from the South African market.

Following independence, the BLS countries attempted to negotiate better terms within the SACU agreement. They sought primarily a greater share of the total revenue and access for their products in the South African market. Small concessions were made by South Africa on the revenue question. In 1969 the total share going to the BLS countries was raised to 2.58%. Swaziland's share of SACU revenue rose from 0.53033% to 0.95%. In 1976 further increases were granted. During the same period South Africa made formal concessions on the access of BLS-produced commodities to the South African market. However, in practice a number of mechanisms continued to exclude all but BLS primary commodities. In return for these concessions, South Africa demanded a greater say in the industrial policies of these countries. In a number of cases it substantially delayed, and at times actually blocked, the establishment of new industrial undertakings in the BLS countries aimed at producing for the South African market.[7]

Under the Botha regime, the SACU agreement is considered a key instrument in South Africa's interventionist regional policy. This policy has as its ultimate objective the creation of a 'constellation of states' linked to and allied with the apartheid regime, whilst isolating and weakening those states committed to loosening ties with South Africa and supporting the liberation struggle in South Africa. To this end the apartheid regime employs both incentives and sanctions against the states of southern Africa. Distribution of revenue under the SACU agreement has now become a means for rewarding or punishing the BLS countries for their behaviour in the region.

This became clear in the mode of distributing SACU revenue for the year 1981–2. South Africa invited the BLS countries to submit their revenue claims according to the 1976 formula. Swaziland claimed R117 million (compared with R52.7 million for the previous year). South African officials replied that this was an overestimation and that the figure should be around R64 million. However, this position was reversed by the South African cabinet which 'noted the error, but accepted the former figure.' An American diplomat described this as 'a R50 million bribe by South Africa to its friends'.

The current phase of SACU renegotiations began in July 1982, and a revenue-sharing formula was agreed upon in October 1982. However, by mid-1984 it had become clear that Pretoria was trying to use this issue to compel the BLS countries, either collectively or individually, to co-operate somehow with its regional 'deconcentration' policy.

Finally, as a landlocked country, Swaziland is virtually totally dependent on South Africa for its external trade. The Maputo rail and road link is its only alternative access to the outside world. As already noted, over 95% of Swaziland's imports arrive in the country through a freight haulage system operated by South African railways. The figure on exports is noticeably lower, as much of Swaziland's major export, sugar, together with some coal, is exported through Maputo. However, far from developing this outlet and so reducing reliance on the South African transport connection, Swaziland has initiated the construction of a new railway. Passing through Swaziland, this 'southern link' will connect the South African town of Komatipoort with the port of Richards Bay, and so permit Swazi goods to be carried to that port.

2. The Tendency to Monoculture
The dependence of the Swazi economy on sugar exports has increased dramatically since 1968. Based on heavy investment

by British capital, particularly by the Commonwealth Development Corporation and Lonrho, sugar production increased from 161,223 tonnes in 1970–1 to 240,695 tonnes in 1979–80. Further expansion brought the total yield to over 400,000 tonnes in 1982–3, making Swaziland Africa's second biggest sugar cane producer.

The sugar industry is the single largest user of land in Swaziland, consumes more water than any other source, and is the largest single employer – it was estimated that 60,000 people were wholly or partly dependent on sugar for a living in 1979. The industry is also a major revenue earner for the government and the single biggest earner of foreign exchange. The contribution of sugar to foreign exchange earnings rose from 20% in 1970 to 50% in 1980 and an estimated 53% in 1983.[8]

Swaziland's annual sugar quota under the Lomé convention stands at 116,400 tonnes. For this it receives a price well above the world average. However, the rest has to be sold at world market prices, which have been in decline since 1980. This has created something of a crisis in Swaziland's balance of payments and government revenue, highlighting the country's dependence on this crop, and the consequent vulnerability of the economy.

3. The Emergence of a Royalist Comprador Bourgeoisie
During the colonial period, the traditional chiefs clustered around the monarchy were confined by the colonial state to pre-capitalist forms of exploitation of the Swazi peasantry. They lived predominantly off forms of tribute exacted from this peasantry and did not emerge in a controlling position within the capitalist economy.[9]

This position has changed dramatically since independence. Through their domination of the political machinery of the state, and predominantly through the institution of the monarchy, the 'traditional' chiefs, and particularly the royal family, have transformed themselves into a comprador bourgeoisie in a tight economic alliance with the mainly South African monopolies which dominate the Swazi economy. This has been achieved largely through an institution known as *Tibiyo Taka Ngwane*. As this is a complex issue it is necessary to go into some detail.

The institutional structure of the Swazi state since independence in 1968 has been built on an implicit but nevertheless clear distinction between the 'Swazi Nation' and the Government of Swaziland. The former refers to so-called 'ethnic Swazis', particularly in designated Swazi Nation land areas, and is organized through the administrative structures of the 'traditional' chieftaincy. The Government of Swaziland is deemed to consist of the 'modern' administrative structures of the Swazi state and is charged with public administration, the economic and social development of the country, and its international relations. The monarch presides over both the Swazi Nation and the Government of Swaziland. However, since independence two separate administrative systems have attempted to control and manage Swaziland's economic resources.

The financial assets of the Swazi Nation consist in the first instance of the actual land holdings in the Swazi Nation areas and the mineral wealth of the country. Both are constitutionally vested under the guardianship of the monarch, and controlled through the traditional institutions of the monarchy rather than the finance ministry of the Government of Swaziland. This ministry, on the other hand, supervises the overall budget of the Swazi state and raises its revenue. However, it does *not* exercise control over the financial assets of the Swazi Nation, and revenue from these does not enter into the annual budget of the Government of Swaziland. This bifurcated system of financial control is crucial to an understanding of the emergence and position of a royalist comprador bourgeoisie through the institution of *Tibiyo Taka Ngwane*, and the struggles which have emerged around it.

The Independence Constitution of the kingdom of Swaziland vested control over the country's mineral wealth in the King, to be held 'in trust' for the Swazi nation. Royalties were paid directly to the monarch. For a period such monies were simply hoarded unproductively in the royal kraal. However, after an attempt to steal some of this money, and on the suggestion of Sishayi Nxumalo, the King established the *Tibiyo Taka Ngwane* Fund (Swazi National Development Fund – hereafter *Tibiyo*) as an investment undertaking based on funds derived from mineral royalties. Through the *Tibiyo* Charter the King charged the fund to 'preserve, in cooperation with such progressive local leadership as is essential to the development of a modern state, the customs and traditional institutions of the Swazi people so as to prevent the disillusionment and instability which has followed from their rapid breakdown in other parts of the world.' *Tibiyo*'s revenue would not accrue to the Ministry of Finance. *Tibiyo* remained under the exclusive control of the monarch and was not accountable to any other branch of the government.

This system was reorganized in 1975. Funds from mineral royalties were now placed under a new organization, *Tisuka Taka Ngwane*. *Tibiyo* itself would begin to act solely as an investment corporation. Its activities were henceforth to be financed by dividend payments from its shareholdings in foreign undertakings in Swaziland and from income generated in various of its other projects. The expenditures of *Tibiyo* are not integrated into the public budget of the Swazi government. Until 1978 *Tibiyo* was able to finance its operating and capital expenditures from its own revenue, which stood at R7 million in that year. However, *Tibiyo*'s large investments since 1978 have significantly exceeded its resources, and the Fund has claimed, and has been granted, substantial funds from the central budget.

The published accounts of *Tibiyo* are sketchy and un-audited. The most recent published are those for 1981. These indicate that in this year *Tibiyo*'s total assets stood at R46,071,573. Its total income for the year 1980–1 was over R10.6 million. Only slightly more than 1% of this income was derived from productive undertakings managed by *Tibiyo*, while just over R2.1 million, or nearly 20%, came from third-party-managed projects. The great bulk of *Tib-iyo*'s income, however, was derived from dividends and interest payments.

Tibiyo's economic power has been consolidated mainly through its shareholdings. In 1981 it held shares in a total of 33 undertakings, including almost all of the largest South African and British undertakings operating in Swaziland. In many cases there existed 'no funds to buy shares of Fund projects'. *Tibiyo*'s holdings in such cases were thus acquired either through being offset against future dividends, through 'loan arrangements with partners', or were granted in return for the provision of Swazi Nation land by *Tibiyo* for the undertaking concerned. In all except one case, *Tibiyo*'s shareholding in these companies ranges between 20% and 50% of share capital. In seven cases it holds over 40% of share capital. Amongst the most important companies in which *Tibiyo* holds shares are the following (*Tibiyo*'s percentage holding is indicated in brackets):

● Havelock Asbestos Mine (40%), owned by the British mining multinational, Turner & Newall, which has operated the lucrative Havelock asbestos mine since 1938;
● Mhlume Sugar Company (50%), jointly owned by *Tibiyo* and the Commonwealth Development Corporation, it operates a sugar plantation and mill with an annual capacity of 145,000 tonnes;
● Royal Swaziland Sugar Corporation (32.4%). The Swazi state has another 32.4% – financed by a R13 million loan from *Tibiyo* – while a consortium of western and African sugar interests holds the remainder. It operates a plantation and mill with an annual capacity of 126,000 tonnes;
● Simunye Plaza (25%), a shopping complex owned by the Kirsch group, based on the Simunye sugar complex;
● Swazispa Holdings (33.4%), owned by the Sun International group. It controls that company's four hotels, its casinos and tourist interests in Swaziland;
● Ubombo Ranches (40%), owned by Lonrho, and connected with the Lonrho Sugar Corporation, in which *Tibiyo* also owns shares.[10]

In addition to the companies in which it holds shares, *Tibiyo* has entered into a joint project with other investors to set up the Royal Swazi National Airlines. Its other activities include:

● land purchases. By 1981 it had spent over R5.2 million in purchasing 'for the Swazi Nation' freehold land held under the 1914 land division. This has now boosted the land area classified as Swazi Nation Land to 57% (compared with 45% at independence). Much of this new land purchased has been used to set up sugar cultivation – both large scale plantations such as Simunye, and two smaller schemes involving a number of small Swazi farmers under the management of the Ubombo Ranches Company;
● educational assistance in the form of various bursaries;
● grants and loans to institutions such as the University of Swaziland, the Swazi Defence Force and various cultural groups.

In a country with limited potential for domestic capital formation, *Tibiyo* has emerged as by far the most important and powerful vehicle for domestic capital accumulation. Two vitally important aspects should be noted here.

Firstly, as stressed above, *Tibiyo*'s revenue and assets do not accrue to the Swazi Ministry of Finance, but are controlled by the traditional rulers organized through the monarchy. *Tibiyo* is accountable neither to parliament nor the Cabinet. Its Board of Trustees is appointed by the monarch. Day-to-day operations are conducted by a Management Committee headed for many years by the former Finance Minister, Sishayi Nxumalo, a close confidant of the late King Sobhuza. Indeed, while Sobhuza was alive Sishayi Nxumalo was widely regarded as the second most powerful man in Swaziland.[11]

Tibiyo has persistently resisted attempts to make it in any way accountable to parliament or to the Cabinet. In 1980 a Commission of Enquiry into corruption was established by Prince Mabandla Dlamini, who was then Prime Minister and also *Tibiyo* chairman. The Commission tried to subpoena the records of *Tibiyo*. Nxumalo appealed to the King against this move, informing him, according to rumour, that the Prime

Minister sought 'to pluck out the hairs of your testicles one by one'. The Commission was closed down.

Despite *Tibiyo*'s fierce resistance to any form of control by the Government of Swaziland, it has not hesitated to demand substantial funds from the public account to mount and sustain its operations. Thus, together with the Swazi Government, *Tibiyo* is the joint owner of the Royal Swazi airlines. Yet in the past five years its R0.75 million injection of funds into the national carrier has been dwarfed by the Government's R17.4 million contribution. Likewise while *Tibiyo* holds one third of the equity of the vast Simunye sugar project, with Government and private investors each holding another third, in 1982–3 the Swazi Government had to inject R10 million into this project and a further R6 million in the following year. The other shareholders have not been required to contribute.

This situation has led to some conflict with officials in the Swazi government, particularly the Finance Ministry. The most glaring example of this occurred in mid-1983. In order to raise external loans *Tibiyo* requested that it be designated by the Government of Swaziland as a National Development Agency. This request was refused on 18 October. The Ministry argued that it would be required to underwrite any loan concluded by *Tibiyo* in a situation in which it had no means of controlling of supervising the Fund's activities. In the words of the Principal Secretary: '*Tibiyo* is not a statutory body under the control of a minister and it has no legal persona which could be the subject of litigation. It cannot therefore satisfy either of the criteria normally applied to issue government guarantees.' One month later a new Swazi cabinet was named in which the *Tibiyo* managing director was appointed Finance Minister. Two days later the Finance Ministry certified *Tibiyo* as a National Development Agency.

Thus, through this exclusive, non-accountable control of the only single local source of money capital, the traditional rulers have used their domination of the institutions of the Swazi state to transform themselves into capitalists. Their material position is now dependent on capitalist forms of exploitation.

Secondly, however, they have done so through an ever closer cooperation, collaboration and alliance with foreign, and particularly South African, capital. The prosperity and material position of this royalist group now rests on the profitable investment of such foreign capital. State power is used to foster the requisite conditions of accumulation for such capital. *Tibiyo* does not itself enter into productive ventures on a significant scale. Rather, it accumulates primarily in rentier fashion through share investments in such undertakings. Thus the material position of the Swazi ruling group is heavily dependent on their collaboration with South African and other foreign capital. They can be characterized as a comprador bourgeoisie in the classic sense of the term. They are able to maintain this position through the royalist control of Swazi politics and the consolidation of traditional institutions.

A Brief Sectoral Analysis

Viewed superficially, economic statistics appear to indicate that the Swazi economy is relatively diversified. In 1981 the manufacturing sector contributed 24% of the country's GDP of R393.37 million (which rose to an estimated R405.5 million in 1982). Agriculture and forestry contributed 23% and the public sector 13%.[12] The manufacturing and the distribution, hotel and restaurant sectors were the two fastest growing sectors in the economy. The relative contribution of the three main sectors to the Swazi GDP in three selected years is shown in Table 1.

A number of aspects are worthy of note here. First is the striking decline in the relative contribution of agriculture to GDP. Secondly, the one quarter share of manufacturing in the Swazi GDP appears to compare favourably with that of highly industrialized societies. However, this figure is misleading and does not indicate a high level of industrialization in Swaziland. A significant proportion of such manufacturing consists of basic processing of two major primary products, sugar and timber. These are included in the industrial census

21

under the categories of food and beverages, and wood and wood products, respectively, and are respectively the largest and second largest Swazi exports. In 1981 the total value of processed sugar exports was slightly over R129 million, while that of wood products was R39.9 million. (Swaziland's third largest export in 1981 was also related to agriculture – fertilizer products, worth R23.6 million. However, in early 1984 the company owning the fertilizer factory was declared bankrupt.)[13] The breakdown of production and employment in the various sectors of manufacturing in 1978–9 is shown in Table 2.

From Table 2 it will be seen that in 1978–9 the two major industrial categories accounted for 54.3% and 24.4% respectively of the total value of manufacturing production, employing respectively 48.2% and 33.9% of the workforce of the manufacturing sector. The processing of wood and sugar apart, manufacturing in Swaziland is confined almost entirely to import substitution undertakings producing for the very small local market. Whilst the Customs Union arrangement is theoretically supposed to allow access of Swazi-manufactured commodities to the far larger South African market, in effect a number of mechanisms have operated to bar from this market manufactured products which compete with South African-produced commodities. The small size of the Swazi market (with a total population of just over 500,000 people) is seen by many capitalists as a brake on expansion. Moreover, in its efforts to attract new industrial investment into Swaziland, the Swazi state confronts severe competition from the wide range of incentives offered by South Africa to industrialists prepared to invest in apartheid's bantustans and adjacent areas. At least one company, Swazi Carpets, has decided to relocate its operations from Swaziland to the Transkei bantustan. Probably even more worrying to the Swazi authorities was the decision in early 1983 by Kirsch Industries to set up a textile factory originally planned for Swaziland in a town bordering the Ciskei bantustan.[14]

The manufacturing sector was the third largest employer of wage labour in both the private and state sectors in 1981. In this year alone there existed 86 manufacturing establishments employing 13,880 persons, of whom 3,548 were women. This workforce accounted for 17.4% of all paid employment in Swaziland, compared with 33.5% in agriculture and 19.5% in social services.[15] The manufacturing workforce is concentrated in relatively large undertakings – 12,205 of its total of 13,880 employees work in establishments employing 100 or more people.[16] A detailed breakdown of distribution of employment by size of undertakings and level of skills is given in Table 3, which shows that in 1981, over 60% of all people employed in the manufacturing sector in Swaziland were working for the 6 largest of the 86 existing undertakings.

Manufacturing apart, three other sectors listed in the industrial census can broadly be said to provide industrial employment. These are mining and quarrying, construction, and electricity and water. Of these, mining and quarrying are entirely in the hands of private companies, whilst electricity and water are controlled by the state. The construction industry is divided between both private and state undertakings.

There are only two relatively large-scale mining operations in Swaziland: the asbestos mine at Havelock, and the Mpaka coal mine. In 1980, Swaziland sold 31,435 tonnes of asbestos and 174,323 tonnes of coal. Coal reserves of at least 200 million tonnes have been discovered. In addition, in 1964 the mining of iron ore for export to Japan was begun. (One consequence of this was the construction of the rail link with Maputo.) However, these reserves were soon exhausted and mining operations stopped in 1977, though the export of stockpiled iron ore continued until 1980. The only other mining operation in the country is a small-scale tin mine at Kubuta.

In 1981, 2,580 people were employed in the four existing mining undertakings. The 33 privately owned construction companies employed 4,345 people, while the state construction sector employed a further 2,409. The state owned electricity and water operation employed 1,453 people in that year. Comparing these three sectors – mining, construction and electricity and water – these employment figures reveal a relatively high concentration into large undertakings in both the mining and construction industries. Average employment

23

in the large mines is well over 500 per undertaking. Likewise in construction, one third of its total workforce in 1981 was employed in just two undertakings, whilst the 12 undertakings employing more than 100 workers each, accounted for 86% of the workforce.[17]

The average monthly wages of semi-skilled and skilled male and female workers in manufacturing, mining, construction and electricity and water are set out in Table 4. This table shows a high degree of variation in wages across sectors.

In terms of contribution to GDP, agriculture is the second largest sector of the Swazi economy (see Table 1). However, this requires closer examination. Conventional analyses of Swazi agriculture employ dualistic models, which distinguish between so-called 'modern' and 'subsistence' sectors. The widespread use of this model derives both from conventional neo-classical bourgeois economics and from the consolidation of such conceptions in the legal land tenure structure of the country. Arising out of the pattern imposed by the specific forms of colonial expansion in Swaziland, the rural areas of the country remain divided into land allocated to individual tenure farms and so-called Swazi Nation land. The former areas were set aside in 1914 for occupation by colonists whilst the latter was 'reserved' for 'ethnic Swazis'. Swazi Nation land is vested in the monarch, 'in trust for the Swazi nation'. In 1914 it accounted for 33% of the total land area. Because of a policy of purchase of individual tenure land by the monarch under the 'buy back' scheme, land classified as Swazi Nation land now accounts for 57% of the total land area.

The conventional dualist analysis of Swazi agriculture describes the economic activities on Individual Land Tenure farms as 'highly modernized' commercial farming, whilst cultivation and stock keeping in the Swazi Nation areas are usually dismissed as 'subsistence production'.[18] However this classification is highly misleading in a number of ways. Firstly, a great deal of Swazi Nation land is now given over to large-scale, intensive, 'modern' sugar cane plantations. Far more fundamentally, however, the category 'subsistence farming' assumes that production on such units is self-contained and somehow outside of the circuits of capital and commodities. Such subsistence farmers are then presumed to be able to satisfy their needs through production in these areas and only leave them when they need to acquire some 'modern' artefact such as a bicycle or a radio. This is historically untrue and completely misrepresents the current situation in these areas. More fundamentally it obscures the crucial fact that peasant family agriculture and capitalist production are, and have been for many decades, inseparably linked and interdependent.

The fact that a large number of individuals producing on this land may not regularly produce a marketable surplus reflects the process of class formation at work in Swazi society. In other words, the relations of production in these areas do not permit the reproduction of labour power through the production and sale on a regular basis of agricultural commodities.

To show this concretely: in 1979–80 there was a total of 57,545 homesteads with a total population of around 400,000 (out of a total 'de facto African population' of 529,605 in 1979). Of these homesteads, 94% reported ownership of land, whilst 65% reported ownership of cattle.[19] In 1977 only 9% of Swazi Nation land was being cultivated, though the World Bank judged that 42% of such land was arable. However, exploitation of such potential arable areas would endanger the national herd, which in 1977 was reported to be grazing on 87% of Swazi Nation land.[20] This extensive grazing was giving rise to acute problems of soil erosion in many areas.

Within the Swazi Nation areas significant differentiation in the patterns of landholding have been established. The 1971–2 Agricultural Sample Census found that 26.5% of all homesteads held less than one hectare of land, and together accounted for a mere 5.5% of the total homestead land areas. On the other hand, 41% of this total land area was held by the 12.2% of homesteads which had land holdings of 5 hectares or more.[21] A rough categorization by a research team from the University of Swaziland Social Science Research Unit identifies three broad types of homestead: 'about one quarter (26.9%) were described as being impoverished or poor; a little more than half (52%) were considered to be of moderate

25

status, composed of buildings made mostly from traditional materials; the remaining fifth (21%) were judged to be showing distinct signs of modernity or wealth'.[22]

Though not satisfactory in itself, such data does point to a significant differentiation in land ownership. More particularly, the families linked with the chiefs can be expected to control larger areas of land. Nevertheless, the average landholding does reveal something of the land shortage confronting the rural population. Such small plots of land are inadequate to engage in the production of agricultural products for sale – they are in fact too small to provide for the reproduction of labour power in general. This would apply even to the 73.5% of homesteads in possession of more than one hectare of land. Thus, according to the 1976 census, only 41% of all households ever sold crops, and only 14% of households in these areas derived an annual income of R500 or more from such rural production.[23] For most households, sales of produce thus made up only a small part of family cash income. Even such surplus-producing families were dependent primarily on the remittances of wages by migrant workers, supplemented by such activities as beer brewing, for cash income.

Residents of the vast majority of homesteads in these areas are thus forced into the regular sale of labour power in order to subsist. In other words, the structure of relations on the land in these rural areas produced a migrant labour force. One study has found that 80% of all rural homesteads had one or more members of the family earning off-farm income – i.e. selling their labour power outside of the Swazi Nation areas. Such absentees amounted to one quarter of the pouplation of these areas in the 1976 census, with a male to female ratio of 3 to 1.[24] This pervasive pattern of ongoing labour migration is not confined to the poorest strata of the rural population, but is rather an integral part of the economic survival of four-fifths of rural dwellers. It can be safely concluded that probably only the small minority of households owning larger tracts of land are able to guarantee their own reproduction through agricultural production in the Swazi Nation areas, and are therefore not obliged to enter the labour market on a regular basis in order to subsist.

The breakdown of the areas of employment of such migrant workers from the Swazi Nation land is interesting. More than three quarters (77.5%) remained in Swaziland, working in urban areas. Just over 17% of the absentees were working in South Africa, with slightly less than half of these employed in the mines (the total number of Swazis working in the South African mines stood at 11,048 in 1981 and has not exceeded 15,000 since 1977).[25]

If the development of agricultural production has led to the increasing proletarianization of the Swazi peasantry on the one hand, it has, on the other hand, seen the consolidation of large-scale capitalist farming dominated by foreign multi-nationals and the few remaining settlers. In this sense the pattern established under colonialism has been further entrenched since independence. The total value of agricultural produce from the individual tenure farms in 1979–80 was just over R58.3 million.

The pattern of land use in the individual tenure areas shows how the production of agricultural commodities is dominated by large-scale producers. In 1979–80 there was a total of 800 individual tenure farms, 483 of which were registered as 'unused holdings'. Of the 317 farms actually in production, just over 90% of the total land in use was accounted for by the 92 farms of more than 1,000 hectares, while the 23 farms of more than 5,000 hectares used 59.9% of such farm land.[26]

These large agricultural undertakings dominate Swazi agricultural production. They employed the vast bulk of the 18,912 people in paid employment in agriculture in 1981.[27] This compares with a 'total active farm population' of 200,397 in the Swazi Nation areas, of whom only 3,548 are paid workers – the balance being categorized as 'unpaid family workers'.[28] The overwhelming bulk of those in agriculture were unskilled workers – only 2,000 were employed in categories other than unskilled. The wages paid to such workers are amongst the lowest in Swaziland. The average monthly earnings of unskilled agricultural workers were R86 for men and R61 for women in 1981.[29] Significantly, the proportion of women in paid employment in agriculture is slightly higher than in any other sector except distribution. Slightly under one third of unskilled workers in agriculture (or 5,357 people) are women. Indeed, one survey of the position of women in paid agricultural labour in Swaziland argues that the large multinational companies which dominate the production of agricultural commodities 'prefer to use female labour because it is supposed to be least "troublesome" '. The appalling conditions of such workers on the plantation of the then British/Swiss-owned company (Libby's) which dominates the production of pineapples, are also highlighted in this survey.[30]

The third major sector of the Swazi economy is that classified as Distribution. This includes the wholesale and retail sectors, together with the hotel and restaurant trade (i.e. effectively including the tourist industry). There is less information available on this sector than on the others – the data is less up to date and less detailed. Nevertheless in 1975–6, 'distribution', so defined, contributed 26.3% of the Swazi GDP, and is seen by the US State Department as one of the fastest growing sectors in the Swazi economy (see note to Table 1).

In 1981 this sector employed 5,682 people.[31] Once again, all three of its component categories – wholesale trade, retail trade, and hotels and restaurants – are dominated by South African monopoly companies. The powerful position of the Kirsch group in both wholesale and retail trade, together with the dominance of the OK Bazaars subsidiary of South African Breweries in the retail sectors, were noted above (p. 11). However, there do exist a number of smaller Swazi-owned operations, particularly in the retail trade, struggling against the domination of South African capital. This sector is the major point of entry for and economic base of small-scale Swazi capitalists. Thus of the 468 registered establishments in the distribution sector in 1981, 299 were operated by working partners and proprietors.[32] Most of these are small Swazi capitalists. Whilst a few of them may have owned small restaurants, the overwhelming bulk were probably operating in the retail sector on the fringes of the urban areas and in the rural areas.

The hotel and tourist sector is almost totally dominated by South African capital. No Swazi-owned hotel operates in the major tourist zone of the country, in the Ezulwini valley between Manzini and the capital, Mbabane, and it can be safely assumed that there are very few in the rest of the country. The profits from the hotel/casino trade – dominated by the Sun International group – are immense, making this probably the most profitable sector of the Swazi economy, and generating in its wake a severe problem of prostitution to satisfy the demands of South Africans for sexual services banned in the apartheid state.

The Current Economic Crisis in Swaziland

Like all other countries in southern Africa, Swaziland is currently in the grip of a severe recession. This is aggravated by the impact of both the recent drought and the cyclone Domoina, which devastated the country in January 1984. In his February 1984 budget speech, the Minister of Finance acknowledged that: 'In economic terms, Swaziland is at present undergoing one of the most difficult periods of its history.'[33] No real growth of GDP had been recorded in the previous two years, compared with growth rates of 10.9% and 7.5% in 1978 and 1981 respectively.[34] There have been a number of spectacular bankruptcies, the most important being that of the giant French-owned fertilizer company, Swaziland Chemical Industries (SCI). This was declared insolvent in March 1984 with debts of R29 million. In 1982, the exports of SCI amounted to R55 million, and this single factory was Swaziland's second biggest foreign exchange earner in that year. It had been planned that the development of SCI would dynamize other industrial enterprises in Swaziland.[35] Moreover, the cost of damage caused by cyclone Domoina to road and rail communications alone was put at R58 million, whilst 'the overall figure may be hundreds of millions'.[36] The extent of the recession is also reflected in the fact that for several years the country has experienced a rising deficit on its balance of payments account. After allowing for the inflow of long- and short-term capital and foreign grants, this deficit reached R63 million in 1983, compared with R15.7 million in 1981.[37]

The recession has had a profound impact on government finances. In 1982–3 the Finance Minister budgeted for a balance of revenue against expenditure. In the event however, a deficit of R33.6 millions was recorded for that year. Similarly, the budgeted 'modest deficit' of R7.1 million for 1983–4 is expected to turn out in practice to be 'only slightly less than that recorded in 1982–3'.[38] The major reason for the growing fiscal crisis of the Swazi state is the dramatic decline in revenue. In particular, government receipts from the sugar export levy declined from a highpoint of R14.3 million in 1980–1 to R1.4 million in the 1983–4 budget. The 1983–4 budget anticipated no government revenue from the sugar industry. Other tax revenue has likewise declined from R38.6 million in 1981–2 to an anticipated R34.3 million in 1983–4. In this context, revenue from the Southern African Customs Union (SACU) – always significant in financing the state budget – is now even more important. Thus the R86.8 million paid in 1980–1 for the year 1979–80, constituted 51% of total state revenue. The R117 million received from SACU as Swaziland's shares of 1981–2 revenue, made up 63% of budgeted government revenue for 1982–3, whilst the R130.4 million received in 1983–4 accounted for 62.5%.[39]

In addition to this, Swaziland has been placed in an adverse competitive position by the exceedingly attractive incentives offered by South Africa under its 'deconcentration' policy to undertakings prepared to establish industrial plants in the bantustans and adjacent areas. As already mentioned, one concern has decided to relocate its operations from Swaziland to the Transkei, while the Kirsch group will now establish a new plant in the Ciskei rather than Swaziland as originally planned.

On its own the Swazi state cannot hope to match the incentives offered to capitalists to invest in the bantustan areas. These incentives include, *inter alia*, low interest capital loans, a period of suspension of taxation, state subsidies of already low wages, preferential railway tariffs and tariff protection. Swaziland could potentially be faced with a withdrawal of industry from its territory, or, at best, the drying up of new industrial investment.

The current recession has severely aggravated a serious problem of unemployment in the country. There are two aspects to such unemployment: structural and cyclical. Even before the current recession assumed its present proportions in Swaziland, it was estimated by Barclays Bank of Swaziland that almost 5,000 additional school leavers were annually entering the ranks of the unemployed – i.e. in the period 1975–80 there were, each year, 5,000 more job seekers than jobs available.[40] With the onset of the full force of the recession, this structural unemployment is being compounded by lay-offs in virtually all sectors. According to the Quarterly Report of the Swazi Central Bank at the end of 1982, more than 2,000 workers had been laid off during that year. This is equivalent to 3.5% of total wage employment in the private sector in 1981. In November 1982 the Minister of Public Works announced that more than 1,000 workers in his department, or 4.5% of the workforce in the public sector, would be laid off in 1983. More such redundancies are planned. In the 1984 budget speech, the Minister of Finance argued that 'it was hard to justify' the existing level of expenditure on personnel in state departments, and referred approvingly to a recent IMF study which concluded that the level of employment in the state sector in Swaziland was 'relatively large . . . compared to similar developing countries'. Ministries are currently working on proposals to shed 'much of the surplus government workforce'.[41]

Clearly such growing unemployment constitutes a threat to the coherence of Swazi society. One index of this was the upsurge in violent armed robberies in 1983 – reaching a level of two a week by the end of the year. In this context, increasing the quota of Swazi migrant labour to South Africa would offer the Swazi government an attractive means of defusing

31

Table 1
Breakdown of Swazi GDP for Selected Years

Sector	1973–4		1975–6		1981	
	R million	*%*	*R million*	*%*	*R million*	*%*
Agriculture & forestry	41.8	42.3	47.1	22.1	90.4	23.0
Manufacturing	22.0	22.2	57.5	26.9	89.6	24.0
Distribution						
Hotels & Restaurants	11.3	11.4	56.3	26.3	n.a.	n.a.
Others	23.9	24.0	52.6	24.7	n.a.	n.a.
Total	*98.9*	*100.0*	*213.5*	*100.0*	*393.37*	*100.0*

Source: For 1973–4 and 1975–6: *Swaziland Annual Statistical Bulletin* (Mbabane) Central Statistics Office, 1980. For 1981: *Economic Review* (Mbabane) Prime Minister's Office, 1982 and *Swaziland Economy in 1981 and Forecast for 1982* (Mbabane) US Embassy, 1982.

Table 2
Output and Employment in Manufacturing in 1978/9

Industrial category	Number of establishments	Value of production (R000)	Number employed
Food & beverages	13	111,246	6,098
Wood & wood products	11	50,057	4,288
Clothing & textiles	8	9,873	600
Paper & paper products	3	4,065	190
Others	22	29,685	1,479
Total	57	204,936	12,655

Source: Swaziland Annual Statistical Bulletin, Table L6, pp 80–2.

Table 3
Distribution of Employment in the Manufacturing Sector by Size of Establishment

No. of employees in under-taking	No. of units	Profes-sional	Adminis-trative	Clerical	Skilled	Semi-skilled	Unskilled	All employees
below 5	14	—	1	1	3	—	17	22
5– 9	7	2	4	6	1	4	28	45
10– 19	16	6	12	19	22	42	119	220
20– 49	16	11	23	54	54	111	273	526
50– 99	12	10	40	72	48	123	569	862
100–249	11	33	73	126	54	128	1,381	1,795
250–499	4	32	17	43	47	135	1,308	1,582
500+	6	139	109	276	364	628	7,312	8,828
Totals:	86	233	279	597	593	1,171	11,007	13,880

Source: Central Statistical Office, *Employment and Wages 1981*, Table A3, p. 31.

Table 4
Average Monthly Earnings of Skilled, Semi-skilled and Unskilled Workers in 1981 (Rand)

Industrial category	Skilled workers		Semi-skilled workers		Unskilled workers	
	M	F	M	F	M	F
Mining	742	—	209	134	181	133
Manufacturing (all)	607	320	177	101	127	104
Food & beverages	716	320	225	130	136	104
Textiles	158	189	150	101	102	75
Wood & wood products	420	—	147	131	98	77
Paper & paper products	209	188	238	70	233	95
Chemical products	689	—	104	—	128	189
Fabricated metals	472	—	244	—	155	195
Other	376	315	170	59	136	149
Construction (private)	404	—	240	94	101	88
(state)	341	—	229	162	79	80
Electricity and water	329	—	258	—	100	110

Source: Central Statistical Office, *Employment and Wages 1981*, Tables 31, 32 & A5, pp. 26, 27 & 33.

the unemployment problem. The number of Swazi workers employed on the South African mines rose by 10% between 1980 and 1981, to reach 11,048. The chief statistician of the Swazi Central Statistics Office expects that the rate of increase doubled in 1981–2. Speculation is now rife that Swaziland could be offered an even greater quota of mine labour by South Africa – perhaps at the expense of other supplier states.

4. An Outline of the Class Structure of Swaziland

No detailed analysis yet exists of the class structure of Swazi society since independence. However, it is possible to draw some broad conclusions.

The '*de facto* African population' of Swaziland in 1980 was given as 547,452. At the time of the 1976 census, very close to two thirds of the population of the country were living in the Swazi Nation areas, while 18% were located on farms in the individual tenure areas and 15% in the urban areas of the country.[42] The majority of the population living in the Swazi Nation areas are conventionally described as 'peasants'. However, even given the pattern of differentiation in land ownership indicated above (p. 25), over 80% of such households are dependent for their existence on the regular sale of the labour power of one or more homestead members in the wage sector at any given moment. This very high incidence of continuous migratory labour outside of these areas, coupled with the low proportion of the population which derives an annual income of R500 or more from production in the Swazi Nation areas – only 14%[43] – suggests that the process of proletarianization of such rural producers is relatively far advanced. Thus, far from constituting a 'peasantry', the large majority of the population of these areas are a semi-proletariat who make up a reserve army of labour for South African capital. Increasingly, they are coming to constitute part of the absolute surplus population which the development of capitalism in southern Africa has scattered across the region.[44]

Turning to those engaged in waged employment, the total

of such persons stood at 79,739 in 1981. This figure included managerial, professional and clerical employees, as well as those engaged in forms of manual labour. Breaking down these figures in an attempt to gauge the size of the Swazi proletariat, the total number of paid employees in all sectors classified in the skilled, semi-skilled and unskilled categories was 72,117 in 1981. When the 11,048 Swazis working on contract on the South African mines is added to this figure, a rough idea emerges of the size of Swaziland's proletariat.[45] Thus although individual conditions vary considerably, and although some of the migrant workers may still retain a measure of access to land in the Swazi Nation areas, there does appear to exist in Swaziland a relatively large proletariat in the classical sense of those 'freed' from the means of production, and 'free' to sell their labour power. Consisting of around 80,000 adult wage labourers (together with their families, of course) this proletariat forms a substantial part of the Swazi population of just over half a million – it comprises just over one third of all Swazis between the ages of 15 and 65, according to the 1976 census.[46]

The size of this proletariat becomes even more significant when it is remembered that the majority of the Swazi population living in the Swazi Nation areas themselves constitute a semi-proletariat, subject to increasing economic pressures driving them off the land. Thus there is a very close connection between these two class forces, the proletariat and the semi-proletariat. But this should not be overstated. There still exist sufficient differences in their objective socio-economic positions and experiences of the processes of capitalist exploitation which act to divide these two related class forces from each other. Thus, for the urban (or plantation) wage labour proletariat, the immediate experience of exploitation is through wage labour. They overwhelmingly confront, as their immediate exploiters, foreign monopoly capital, both South African and British. The Swazi state appears as the defender of such foreign monopoly capital. Indeed, as the quotation cited above (p. 10) shows, it is a major objective of this state to prevent the effective combination of the Swazi proletariat in a struggle against their exploitation by such capital. In this sense then, the governing royalist alliance which controls *Tibiyo* and the apparatuses of the Swazi state confronts the Swazi proletariat as the ally of foreign (and often South African) monopoly capital, and seeks to prevent the organization of Swazi workers in order to advance both its own position and that of its monopolist allies.

However, for the semi-proletariat living in the Swazi Nation areas, whatever the objective similarities of their position to that of the proletariat, the experience of the impact of capitalist exploitation differs in ways which significantly affect their actual and potential political practice. For this semi-proletariat, the prime impact of capitalist exploitation is not directly and constantly experienced through the wage labour relation. For those working on the land, their declining living standards, their inability to reproduce their labour power, does not appear as the direct result of the operations of foreign multinational companies, but rather as a shortage of land and cattle. Such producers are not *directly* confronted with monopoly capital as their immediate exploiters and oppressors. Even for those who engage in fairly regular, if interrupted, bouts of migrant labour outside these areas, the factor propelling them into such labour appears as a shortage of land and cattle, rather than the private ownership of the means of production by monopoly capital.

All of this has important, if contradictory, effects for the political stance of this semi-proletariat. In Swaziland, access to land in these areas is controlled by the 'traditional' chiefs, operating under the umbrella of the institutions of the monarchical system. Although there is almost no information on this point, it is clear that some form of surplus has to be paid to the chiefs in return for the 'right' to use the land. Moreover, various 'traditional' ceremonies, such as that of the first fruits, also ensure a flow of surplus labour from all such households in Swaziland to the kraal of the monarch. Thus, at one level, it could be argued that at the level of daily experience it is the chiefs and the monarchical system which appear as the immediate exploiters and oppressors of this rural population.

However, such appearances are offset by more pressing aspects of this system of production relations. Firstly, the ideological cement of 'tradition' still remains strong – the levels of surplus extraction by the chiefs and monarch through this form do not appear to give rise to extreme forms of social differentiation in the Swazi Nation areas such as would lead to popular resistance against these ruling groups. More importantly however, since the division in 1914 of the territory of the then British Protectorate of Swaziland into Swazi Nation land (one third of the total land area) and individual ternure farms (two thirds), the Swazi monarchy – presided over by the late King Sobhuza II for all but 9 years of this period – has concentrated its efforts on reclaiming for the Swazi Nation as much as possible of the land expropriated by colonialism. This should not be misunderstood. The monarch and the chiefs have *not* led a popular struggle to reclaim stolen land. Rather, they have operated strictly through negotiation and land purchase. Nevertheless, this central emphasis given to reclaiming 'traditional' Swazi land for 'the nation', has directly affected the political practice of the Swazi semi-proletariat. Thus if the shortage of land appears to this class force as the major cause of its increasing impoverishment, the very emphasis given to the land question by the chiefs and the apparent attempts to reclaim Swazi land for the nation has won widespread support from the majority of the inhabitants of the Swazi Nation areas. It has in fact consolidated the political hold of the chiefs over these areas through the traditional councils called the *Tinkundla* in which are represented all adult males of a particular area. Thus it could be argued that the political support given by the semi-proletariat to the traditional chiefs is institutionalized through the *Tinkundla*, consolidating even further the traditionalist and monarchist ideology which has such a powerful hold in Swaziland, particularly in the rural areas.[47] This differential experience of the impact of capitalist exploitation between the urban proletariat and the semi-proletariat in the rural areas has been a significant factor inhibiting the emergence of a mass popular movement in Swaziland. At crucial moments, when such an alliance appeared a possibility, the intervention of the monarchy against the struggles of the proletariat, and its manipulation of the land question to win the support of the rural population, has in fact isolated the Swazi working class from the mass of the population. The clearest example of this was the round of strikes in 1962–3.

This points to the third major class force in Swazi society, which is in fact a differentiated bloc of the 'traditional' rulers operating under the monarchy. The constitution of this traditional bloc is complex and requires much further research. At its head stands the royal family presided over by the monarch – either the King or Queen Regent. Swazi royalty consists of the monarch, the numerous lineage descendants of the Swazi Kings, together with the 'elders of the Nation'. The latter are the hereditary heads of the major clans of Swaziland, of whom three have a greater weight than the rest, and the spokesman of whom is known in English as 'The Authorized Person'. The King (or Queen Regent) and the elders together constitute the Swazi monarchy. While the King is the most powerful member of the monarchy and enjoys a wide range of discretionary powers, his powers are not unlimited. The elders collectively have the right to check, and at times reverse, the actions of the King. This system of checks and balances within the monarchy is real and crucial to an understanding of the operation of 'traditional power' in the Swazi kingdom.

Below the elders stand the *Indunas* and the chiefs. The *Indunas* do not inherit their position. Rather they are councillors and administrators appointed by the monarch and elders. Together with certain chiefs, some of the more prominent *Indunas* are grouped together in an advisory council to the monarchy known as the *Liqoqo*. The chieftancies are hereditary positions, in which major chiefs have jurisdiction over minor chieftancies. The precise number of chieftancies in Swaziland is not known, but all chieftancies are organized by the elders into sixteen major groupings, on which are based the *Tinkundla*. The entire traditional bloc of royalty, *Indunas* and chiefs are also organized into an institution known as the *Libandla* (usually translated as the 'Swazi national council'). Collectively the traditional bloc organized through the monarchy constitutes the most powerful set of indigenous class forces in Swaziland.

The power of this traditional ruling class is derived first of all from their control over the basic means of production for the majority of the Swazi population – land. While in theory land is usually communally owned by the Swazi nation, effective control is vested in this group, and land may be disposed of by them. This control of land has secured the total dominance of this bloc in Swazi politics since the 1960s. In turn, this political dominance, and control over certain key apparatuses of the Swazi state since independence, has been the vital factor permitting the transformation of its objective position. It should be repeated here that through the monarchy and the *Tibiyo Taka Ngwane* fund, the traditional ruling bloc has latched onto the coat tails of foreign monopoly capital and transformed itself (or elements of itself) into a comprador royalist bourgeoisie. The crucial political institution now maintaining their control over the Government of Swaziland is the *Liqoqo*, which has been eleveated by the elders to what is now termed the 'supreme council of state'.

The central political role of the *Liqoqo* is analysed below (p. 51). Here however it should be noted that some of its members are commoners. This points to an important development in the alliances made by the royalist comprador bourgeoisie since independence. Basically, in order to consolidate its power and to give a veneer of modernity to its rule, this traditional ruling bloc has, since the 1960s, incorporated a small but important section of the Swazi petty bourgeoisie and intelligentsia into its institutions of economic and political power. Together with the monarchy and the traditional chiefs, this educated stratum originating in the petty bourgeoisie completes what may be termed the governing royalist alliance. Its power is consolidated at various levels in a wide variety of institutions throughout Swazi society and is sustained through the pervasive official ideology of royalism.

The final significant class force of Swazis is the petty bourgeoisie. This term includes on the one hand small capitalists and petty commodity producers, and on the other hand wage earners and professionals who occupy posts allocated to relatively educated persons in the mental/manual divion of labour. This second category would include groups such as lawyers, teachers, clerks, state officials, etc. Given the state of Swazi statistics, the size of this class force is difficult to estimate. Some indication of the number of small Swazi capitalists is given on p. 28 above. Employment statistics reveal that in 1981 a total of 12,030 Swazi citizens were employed in all public and private sectors in the professional and technical, managerial and administrative, clerical, and related categories. Of this group, 8,138 were employed by the state, more than 3,000 of them in education.[48] The current fiscal crisis of the Swazi state is placing the position of elements of this stratum in some jeopardy.

In an economy dominated by foreign monopolies and a monarchical state under the rigid political control of the governing royalist alliance, this petty bourgeoisie is subject to complex and contradictory pressures. The high level of corruption in Swazi society affects them all.[49] More particularly, the closely guarded system of patronage operates to the detriment of small Swazi capitalists who face extreme competitive pressures from more cost efficient monopoly undertakings. This generates widespread popular support for policies such as those of the former Prime Minister, Prince Mabandla Dlamini, who clearly sought to use the office of the Prime Minister to weaken the stranglehold of the *Tibiyo* faction over Swazi politics and to attack corruption. On the other hand, however, it leads to intense individualism and scrambling for positions within and through the state apparatus. The way to advance in Swazi society is through the structures created by the royalists, and this has produced an opportunist royalism in elements of this class force. As seen above, some of its leading members have in fact succeeded in insinuating themselves into the governing royalist alliance.

Such conditions have not been conducive to the formation of a popular alliance between the petty bourgeoisie and the exploited classes of Swazi society. While the virtual total foreign, particularly South African, domination of the Swazi economy might be expected to produce a form of economic nationalism in reaction, the very close links maintained between the Swazi ruling class and foreign monopoly capital make such a stance both economically and politically unproductive (at best) in the short term, for the Swazi petty bourgeoisie. Nevertheless, recent political manoeuvrings by the royalists, as well as the growing economic insecurity of lower strata of the petty bourgeoisie, have produced some signs of disaffection at various levels in the period since the death of King Sobhuza.

The ultimate dominant class in Swaziland is in fact not Swazi. As indicated above, the country is subject to South African economic, and less directly, political, domination – whilst British monopoly capital also controls significant sectors of the economy. Such foreign monopoly capitalists constitute the real dominant class in Swaziland. However, they sustain this dominance through co-operation with the economic and political aspirations of the governing royalist alliance.

5. Political Struggles Since Independence

Swaziland gained its independence in 1968 as a constitutional monarchy. It was ruled by a Cabinet drawn from the ruling party in a parliament elected by universal franchise. The King was head of state. Constitutionally he retained few executive powers, but in reality Sobhuza exercised effective political power within the parameters of the monarchical system described above (p. 41).

In the pre-independence elections of 1967, the King's party – the Imbokodvo National Movement – won all the seats in parliament, largely because of the overwhelming support for the INM from the Swazi Nation areas. However, the opposition Ngwane National Liberatory Congress, which represented the radical petty bourgeoisie and had strong support in the working class, won 20% of the vote.

Independence was followed by vigorous measures to disrupt trade union organization and other forms of popular combination. Works' councils and various forms of industrial conciliation were introduced in an attempt to forestall the emergence of effective trades unions. After 1973, meetings of more than ten people required official permission – and this has often been denied to working class organizations. This attack on the organizations of the working class produced a clear political response. In the 1972 elections working class disaffection was a major factor behind the NNLC's victory in three constituencies which contained a high concentration of workers. This resulted in the unseating of the then Minister of Commerce, Prince Mfanasibili Dlamini, who was also the accepted leader of the lineage which expected to provide the eventual successor to King Sobhuza.

The election of NNLC members of parliament was seen as a direct challenge to the ruling alliance, and an 'insult' to the King. Moreover, the humiliating defeat of Mfanasibili disturbed the delicate relations within the royal family.[50] The governing party in effect refused to accept the elected NNLC members in parliament and a number of crude manoeuvres were made to exclude them. When these were finally ruled unconstitutional by the Swazi High Court in 1973, the dominance and legitimacy of the monarchy was seen to be under challenge. The King thus declared a State of Emergency, dismissed parliament, and dissolved all political parties including his own. All legislative, executive and judicial power was now assumed by the monarchy. At the same time the King announced the establishment of a national army in order to create an armed force exclusively responsible and loyal to the monarch, and capable of suppressing any form of popular resistance – King Sobhuza was reputedly concerned about the loyalty of the police force. The King's coup was carried out in the name of Swazi tradition. It was argued that a Westminster type of parliament was an un-Swazi institution and encouraged disloyalty to the King.

The King ruled by decree from 1973 to 1978. Apart from banning all political parties, action was taken to weaken the remaining trade unions. One – the Swaziland National Union of Teachers – was banned outright. Of the nine registered trades unions in existence in 1970, only one survived at the time of King Sobhuza's death in 1982 – the small and petty-bourgeois oriented Bank Workers' Union. Other repressive measures were introduced, including detention without trial. Fifteen opposition and trade union leaders were detained for long periods. These included Dr Ambrose Zwane, leader of the NNLC, and the leading figure in the 1962–3 strikes, Prince Dumisa Dlamini. These measures, though relatively mild by some standards, succeeded in breaking the opposition and depoliticizing the Swazi masses.

The New Institutional Structure After 1978

In 1978 the King considered the situation sufficiently under control to introduce a new constitution – described as a mixture of Swazi tradition and Western democracy. This new constitutional structure contained a number of important institutions, viz: parliament, the Cabinet, the *Libandla*, the *Liqoqo*, and the monarchy.

Under this system, parliament was 'elected' through the traditional structures known as the *Tinkundla* in such a way that it is entirely nominated by the King.[51] At the same time, a Prime Minister and Cabinet were appointed by the monarch from amongst the members of parliament. Under this new constitution, parliament and Cabinet were not centres of real political power. The Cabinet of ministers was effectively a purely administrative body which ran the civil service, and oversaw the implementation of policies decided upon elsewhere. As a handpicked body of traditionalists, parliament was intended to legitimate the decisions of the monarchy. Criticism in parliament was intended to be directed only at the administrative structures (Cabinet and ministries) rather than at the real policy-making institutions. Real power remained in the hands of the monarchy.

The *Liqoqo* functioned as the executive of the Swazi National Council – the so-called *Libandla* – composed of all the chiefs and members of the royal family. However the *Libandla* seldom met, and functioned largely to ratify decisions already made. The *Liqoqo* was appointed exclusively by the King and elders. Its membership remained secret. The monarchy and the *Liqoqo* were the real policy-making bodies in Swaziland. Thus real politics were confined to the royalist institutions. Differences within the ruling class had to be fought out within the framework of these institutions.

Through this institutional set up, the governing royalist alliance of traditional bloc and a section of the petty bourgeoisie maintained their control over the apparatuses of the Swazi state. Nothing resembling a popular group opposed to their rule emerged after the banning of the NNLC and the

47

smashing of the trades unions. However this ruling royalist alliance was replete with contradictions, generating a series of acute tensions and increasingly bitter factional struggles within it. This political power struggle within the governing royalist alliance was, and remains, essentially a squabble for personal position. It did not reflect any profound ideological divisions or major strategic differences. After 1978 the scramble for position and political conflict centred around the potential succession to the aging King. While Sobhuza was alive, his position was inviolate and the factional struggles remained to some extent hidden within the complex rituals of royalism. Well aware of this politicking, Sobhuza skilfully played off faction against faction. However, with his death in August 1982 the conflicts between them burst into the open, and began to undermine the institutional structure so carefully erected by Sobhuza.

Factional Struggles in the Swazi State[52]

Four phases in this factional struggle after 1978 can be identified. In each case the relationship between the various institutions of the new constitutional set-up became a focus of conflict.

a) From the New Constitution to the Death of the King, 1978–March 1982:

In November 1979, the then Swazi Prime Minister, Prince Maphevu, died. King Sobhuza appointed Prince Mabandla Dlamini to the vacant post. Mabandla's appointment was significant for a number of reasons. Firstly, although he is the eldest son of one of the kingdom's elders, prior to his appointment Mabandla had not been openly involved in Swazi politics, but managed a sugar plantation. His appointment was thus seen as the bringing in of a figure untainted by corruption, and uninvolved in the factional struggle. Secondly, soon after taking office, Mabandla appointed a Commission of Enquiry into Corruption. He could only have done so with the approval of the King. This step was very popular in Swaziland. A number of prosecutions were brought involving the relatives of prominent royalists. However, it seems clear that the Commission was initially intended only to investigate corruption in the ministries, and not in the crucial structures of royalist power. It also seems clear that Mabandla began to use this Commission to attack the power of certain key royalists, associated with *Tibiyo Taka Ngwane* (of which institution, as Prime Minister, Mabandla was *ex-officio* chairman). When the Commission began to subpoena the files of *Tibiyo*, the royalists fought back. The Managing Director of *Tibiyo*, Sishayi Nxumalo, persuaded King Sobhuza to close down the Commission in August 1980, declaring that it had 'acted like the police'. Mabandla described this as 'a defeat'.

Mabandla had gained further popularity by unfreezing Swaziland's relations with Mozambique, and making certain limited attempts to bring Swaziland's foreign policy into line with that of other OAU members. However, this position was weakened when the King appointed one of his main opponents, R. V. Dlamini, as Foreign Minister. The limits to Mabandla's attempts to initiate a more flexible Swazi regional policy have been clearly revealed, firstly by the fact that, as is now known, Mabandla himself was Swaziland's signatory to a then secret non-aggression pact with South Africa in February 1982, and secondly that, despite Mabandla's strong opposition, the Swazi government entered into negotiations with Pretoria over the possible cession by the apartheid regime to Swaziland of two bantustan areas of South Africa – the so-called 'land deal'.[53]

Thus even before the death of the King, the line-up of forces in the factional struggle was becoming clear. It is difficult to identify the forces coalescing around Mabandla. Yet it would seem that he won the support of elements of the Swazi petty bourgeoisie which were not directly incorporated into the royalist alliance, and which did not directly benefit from the extensive patronage network. These forces tried to use the Prime Minister's Office and the Commission of Enquiry into Corruption in an attempt to weaken the royalist element and gain access to the profits, privileges and patronage over which the royalists had hitherto retained a tight monopoly. Yet all these political battles had to be fought out behind a declaration of total support for the King. It was impossible to attack Sobhuza's position or the traditionalist royalist system openly. Thus the Mabandla group remained relatively weak. This was seen very clearly when their opposition to the land deal – mainly on security grounds – was stifled.

b) August 1982–March 1983
The death of the 83-year-old King Sobhuza in August 1982 created a major power vacuum. Sobhuza's chosen heir was the 16-year-old Prince Makhosetive. According to Swazi tradition, his appointment as heir apparent was not publicly announced. The appointment of a minor as heir apparent was also in keeping with Swazi tradition. It is a practice whereby the old King is not obliged finally to favour any of the competing factions by choosing his heir from among the Princes in their ranks. This gives the factions time to fight out their battle for dominance before the heir assumes the throne at the age of 21. In the interregnum the *Indlovukazi* (literally, 'she elephant' – the Queen Mother) would preside over the monarchy as Regent. In order to avoid a situation in which the Queen Mother (Regent) would involve herself in the factional struggle to advance the position of her own son, Sobhuza named as Queen Regent the childless Princess Dzeliwe. This too was in keeping with Swazi tradition.

The contradictions in the Swazi ruling class, to some extent held in check under the King, erupted into fierce and open factional conflicts after his death. These struggles for factional and personal power centred around the institutional structure which Sobhuza erected to handle the succession. In the absence of any effective movement of the popular masses, these conflicts have been the dominating feature of Swazi politics following Sobhuza's death.

In order to grasp the changing forms which this struggle has taken, it is important to understand first the formal structure of power which emerged after the King's death.

There were in fact three distinct power centres:

- the monarchy: headed by the Queen Regent Dzeliwe, and including the 'Authorized Person' Prince Sozisa, and the other elders of the nation.
- the *Liqoqo*. Following Sobhuza's death, the *Liqoqo* was transformed into a public body, and its role elevated by the elders. Its members began to receive state salaries. It later came to be officially described as 'the Supreme Council of State'. The position of the Queen Regent, the Authorized Person, and the *Liqoqo* in relation to each other soon gave rise to conflict.
- the Cabinet and parliament. After August 1982, the subordinate position of the Cabinet, and to a lesser extent, parliament, came to be challenged by one of the contending factions.

The emerging factional struggle in the post-Sobhuza period has sometimes been characterized in press reports as a conflict between different institutions (the 'modern' Cabinet versus 'traditional' *Liqoqo*). In fact, more correctly, it was both a struggle between different class factions present in both sets of institutions and a squabble for personal power within and across these factions. In broad terms, the main factions can be seen as on the one hand those sections of the Swazi traditional aristocracy and petty bourgeoisie who had a stake in the capitalist sector through such institutions as *Tibiyo*, and on the other hand those sections of the Swazi petty bourgeoisie supported by a minority of the traditional aristocracy favourable to capitalism, but themselves without such an institutional stake.

As already indicated, *Tibiyo* served as a major vehicle for capital accumulation by sections of the Swazi royalist alliance. At the end of April 1981, its assets were valued at over R46 million. These consisted mainly of large shareholdings in most of the major capitalist enterprises in the country as well as substantial land holdings. It was clearly in the interest of those class forces most closely linked with *Tibiyo* to maintain the structure of royalist power in which institutions like the Fund benefit from a high degree of official patronage, whilst at the same time being free from control by government departments. These forces maintained close links with South African capital (now dominant in all sectors except agriculture and banking). They generally favoured maintaining, or even deepening, Swaziland's economic links with South Africa. The group also inclined towards closer political links with South Africa, both on the land deal question and on security issues. Significantly, following the South African raid against the ANC in Maseru, Lesotho, in December 1982 (in which 42 men, women and children were massacred, including 12 Lesotho citizens) the Swazi Foreign Minister, a leading member of the *Tibiyo* faction, did not condemn the brutal attack. Rather he said that this 'tragedy' showed what happened when there was a lack of dialogue in the region, and that it justified Swaziland's position of non-interference in the affairs of neighbouring states. The group was behind the strong security clampdown on the ANC in Swaziland around this time.

The leading personalities in this faction were Sishayi Nxumalo, managing director of *Tibiyo*, and Prince Mfanasibili Dlamini. Sishayi Nxumalo has been described by one American diplomat as a shrewd and highly intelligent man, who is also very ambitious and would like to become 'emperor' of Swaziland. Nxumalo was not, however, a member of the *Liqoqo*. Prince Mfanasibili, apart from being a *Liqoqo* member, is the acknowledged leader of the lineage from which the heir to the throne has been drawn. He thus regards himself as the guardian of the monarchy. His major allies in the *Liqoqo* are Chief Mfanawenkhosi Maseko and George Msibi (the latter being the spokesman of the Swazi nation on the joint Boundary Commission established with South Africa to investigate the land deal). This faction was also strongly represented in the Cabinet, where its leading spokespeople were Justice Minister Polycarp Dlamini and Foreign Minister Richard Velaphi Dlamini.

The other faction was less coherently organized than the

first, and less well represented in the royalist institutions. However, it broadly favoured reducing the role and influence of *Tibiyo* by placing it under the control of, and making it accountable to, government departments (in which this faction was better represented). It also favoured a tightening up of overt forms of corruption. It sought a foreign policy in which Swaziland was less openly aligned with South Africa. This became apparent particularly in its opposition to the land deal and in its approach towards South African refugees in Swaziland (whom the apartheid regime wanted controlled and even expelled from the Kingdom). Thus the large-scale round-up of ANC refugees in December 1982 was undertaken by the security forces without consulting the responsible minister – the Deputy Prime Minister, Senator Nsibanze – who offered his resignation on this issue. He was persuaded by Mabandla to remain in office. In the end, many of the announced security measures were not enforced. The leading personalities of this faction were: Prime Minister Mabandla, and Prince Gabheni – a direct son of Sobhuza, member of the *Liqoqo* and Minister of Home Affairs. The then Deputy Prime Minister, Senator Ben Nsibandze, was also said to have been broadly in favour of Mabandla's policies, although not openly aligned with him.

As indicated above, rivalries between these factions had already surfaced before Sobhuza's death, but were held in check by the King's skilful balancing of one against the other and the ideological hold he had over both. After the King's death the first move in the power struggle came from the *Tibiyo* faction which prompted attempts to give the *Liqoqo* (in which it was strongly represented) power and status. It was also responsible for a number of early efforts to limit the power of the Prime Minister by excluding him from any significant role in the ceremonies surrounding Sobhuza's funeral and the succession by the Queen Regent. So apparently successful were these early manoeuvres, that a number of informed observers originally anticipated that resistance to the *Tibiyo* faction would largely come from within the *Liqoqo*, with Prince Gabheni as the focal personality. In the event however, the counter moves from this faction emerged largely from the office of the Prime Minister in the early part of 1983.

The details of this are difficult to unravel as they were based mainly on rumour and speculation. However it is known that on 2 February, Prince Mfanasibili and Chief Maseko were provoked into warning the Queen Regent that Mabandla and the police (under the jurisdiction of Gabheni's Home Affairs Ministry) were planning a coup. This was followed by a series of rumours over the next nine days that the Prime Minister had attempted to sideline Justice Minister Polycarp Dlamini by having him appointed Ambassador to the United States. The move was apparently endorsed by the Queen Regent. However, it was blocked by the combined efforts of Foreign Minister R. V. Dlamini and members of the *Liqoqo*, who argued that the Supreme Council of State was being by-passed by the Prime Minister. On 10 February 1983, amidst rumours of a coup, a detachment of police was sent to guard the Prime Minister's residence, and road blocks were erected around the capital, Mbabane. The next move was a bizarre incident the following day in which a leopard, which had supposedly just wandered into the Prime Minister's residence, was shot by a police marksman. The leopard skin was hastily presented by Mabandla to the Queen Regent – a thinly disguised attempt to take advantage of the Swazi custom under which this privilege is granted only to the closest confidants of the monarch. Throughout the same month Mabandla threatened to revive the Corruption Commission, leading one pro-*Tibiyo* member of Parliament to label the Prime Minister a 'persecutor'.

In the course of these manoeuvres, Mabandla is said to have won the ear but not the total support of the Queen Regent. It is also said that there was support for the Prime Minister and his policies among senior police commanders. The anti-corruption stance undoubtedly had a certain popular appeal among sections of the Swazi population. However, Mabandla never managed to consolidate an effective, organized political base – at least, none sufficient to challenge the *Tibiyo* faction. His politics remained those of the cabal and intrigue within the palace. One indication of this was that no other member of the Cabinet was openly allied with him, although several were broadly sympathetic to his policies.

However, Mabandla finally overplayed his hand in a manoeuvre which his rivals could present as an attack on the *Liqoqo* and the basic institutions of the monarchy. After a month of intrigue, Prince Mfanasibili and Chief Maseko, the two important *Liqoqo* members who had made allegations against Mabandla and the police to the Queen Regent in the presence of three other *Liqoqo* members, were arrested and charged with making 'seditious statements relating to the police'. Mabandla later intervened with the Chief Justice to prevent the two being released on bail pending their trial on 21 March. The prosecution opposed bail on the grounds that Mfanasibili and Maseko might 'interfere' with the three other *Liqoqo* members who were subpoenaed to give evidence against them.

In effect, through this trial, Mabandla clearly hoped to force a split in the *Liqoqo* by requiring three of its members to turn on another two. Such an open attack on both a basic institution of royalist political power and the leading figure in the legitimate royal lineage (Prince Mfanasibili) could not be tolerated. After a weekend of great confusion, Mabandla was dismissed from the premiership the day before the trial was due to begin. His dismissal, and the dropping of all charges against Mfanasibili and Maseko, were clearly the result of strong pressure from major forces within the monarchy. Mabandla's intervention to prevent the accused being released on bail was presented as interference with the courts, whilst the charge itself was said to have been an attempt to muzzle the supreme council of state. Mabandla had clearly overreached himself. No member of the *Liqoqo* could afford to be seen to be associated with such an attack on the integrity of one of the basic institutions of the Swazi monarchical system. This move left Mabandla isolated from his major allies. Prince Gabheni was one of the *Liqoqo* members present at the announcement of Mabandla's dismissal, thus being seen to be politically associated with this measure.[54]

Amidst reports in the South African press that Mabandla might be charged with treason, the ex-Prime Minister fled to South Africa. His successor as Prime Minister was named as Prince Bekhimpi Dlamini, previously deputy minister in the Deputy Prime Minister's office. At the time of his appointment he was described as 'a conservative traditionalist'. The Authorized Person later claimed that Bekhimpi had been the first to suggest to King Sobhuza that Swaziland should 'get our land back from South Africa' and that this began the negotiations over the land deal.[55]

c) March–September 1983
The dismissal of Mabandla on 20 March 1983 was an important victory for the *Tibiyo* faction. Yet it did not end the factional conflict. Influential figures who had broadly supported Mabandla's policies continued to hold important offices in the Swazi state. These included the Queen Regent Dzeliwe, Home Affairs Minister and *Liqoqo* member Prince Gabheni, and the Deputy Prime Minister, Ben Nsibandze. The Queen Regent in particular still retained significant discretionary powers under the monarchical system. The most important of these in this particular phase of the factional conflict was the right to nominate candidates, first for the electoral college, and then for the list from which the members of parliament are chosen. Given that before Mabandla's dismissal it was announced that elections would be held some time in 1983, the manner in which the Queen Regent would exercise her powers of nomination became an important issue in the factional struggle. Dzeliwe was known to be sympathetic to Mabandla and on a number of occasions had shown that she would not function as a mere rubber stamp for the *Liqoqo*.[56] Thus, in order to consolidate its position, the *Tibiyo* faction clearly had to bring the Queen Regent to heel. Following Mabandla's dismissal, the position of the Queen Regent became the crucial issue in the factional conflict.

Indications soon emerged that the dominant faction in the *Liqoqo* sought to diminish the stature and the role of Dzeliwe. On a number of state and ceremonial occasions, when it had previously been announced that she would officiate, Dzeliwe was replaced at the last minute by the Authorized Person, Prime Minister Bekhimpi, the Governor of the Lobamba Royal Residence, or some other official more acceptable to the dominant bloc within the *Liqoqo*.

The campaign against Dzeliwe came to a head in July and August 1983. There were two main reasons for this. Firstly, top level secret negotiations between the Swazi and South African governments over the land deal were continuing – despite the fact that the issue had been referred to a Commission of Enquiry and was technically *sub judice*. This was revealed in a leaked letter from the Acting Administrative Secretary of the *Liqoqo* to the Prime Minister. Dated 28 June 1983, this letter named an eight-member Swazi delegation to be led by the Foreign Minister and referred to the 'secret nature of the negotiations'. Given the sensitive character of these negotiations, and the great importance attached to the successful conclusion of the land deal by the dominant faction in the *Liqoqo*, it was clearly in this group's interest at this time to reduce as far as possible the influence of those groups in the Swazi state opposed to the land deal. The opposition of the loosely organized Mabandla faction to this land deal has now been documented by the *Liqoqo*. Its three-page pamphlet entitled *Mabandla's Litany of Betrayal* makes clear that Mabandla had opposed the land deal before both the King and Cabinet since at least June 1982, leading the *Liqoqo* to pose the hyperbolic question: 'what greater Treason has ever been committed by a Prime Minister in the entire history of civilized mankind?'[57]

The second reason for the intensification of the campaign against Dzeliwe was linked to the forthcoming elections. A *Times of Swaziland* reporter was detained in late July for reporting that the elections would be held in October. The election date had previously only been announced to the *Liqoqo* and was not yet public knowledge. It was widely believed that the source of this leak was Prince Mfanasibili. His motives are thought to have been an attempt to ensure that the elections were actually held on that date, as he judged the moment ripe for the *Tibiyo* faction. Queen Dzeliwe, on the other hand, appeared to favour postponing the elections in the hope of asserting her authority over the *Liqoqo*. It was widely rumoured at the time that Mabandla had secretly returned to Swaziland to discuss strategy with Dzeliwe, and there is some evidence that she was considering restoring him to the premiership.

These conflicts reached their climax at a meeting between Dzeliwe and the *Liqoqo* on 2 August. Here Dzeliwe was presented with a document transferring many of her powers to the Authorized Person. This she refused to sign and announced her intention to dismiss the *Liqoqo*. However, before she could do so, the *Liqoqo* (or at least some members of it) presented her with a statement of her own dismissal which they insisted that she should sign. On the advice of a close aide Dzeliwe refused to comply, and the statement of her dismissal was eventually signed by the Authorized Person, Prince Sozisa, and published in the *Government Gazette* on 9 August.

This manoeuvre provoked a swift response from the remaining influential figures associated with the loosely organized 'Mabandla faction', whose own positions were now also under threat. Led by Home Affairs Minister and *Liqoqo* member Prince Gabheni, they summoned a meeting of the 'Swazi nation' (in fact chiefs) at the Lobamba Royal Residence to discuss the unconstitutional dismissal of Dzeliwe, claiming that most chiefs supported Dzeliwe. This step was a direct challenge to the dominant bloc in the *Liqoqo*. The Lobamba Residence is the seat of royal power, and the fact that the meeting was called there indicated that significant opposition to Dzeliwe's dismissal existed among sections of the chieftancy.

The challenge was met by an order signed by the Prime Minister and the Authorized Person declaring that the Lobamba meeting would be interpreted as an act of rebellion and dealt with accordingly. Chiefs attempting to attend the meeting were turned back by the army. Dzeliwe then instituted an action in the High Court to have the dismissal order declared null and void. However a few days before judgement was due to have been delivered, the Authorized Person issued an extraordinary decree that the court was incompetent to pronounce on this issue. This order was grudgingly accepted by Chief Justice Nathan, who nevertheless complained that it breached a specific undertaking given to the Court, and considerably reduced the power of the judiciary in Swaziland. Shortly thereafter Dzeliwe's lawyer was detained, joining in prison Arthur Khoza, a former interpreter for King Sobhuza, Permanent Secretary in the Ministry of Agriculture and the man who advised Dzeliwe not to sign her dismissal order.

A spate of further detentions followed. These included prominent members of the royal family close to Dzeliwe, amongst them the Assistant Minister in the Deputy Prime Minister's office, Prince Sulumlomo, and Prince Thunduluka. A detention order was also signed by the Prime Minister against Prince Gabheni. However, on the only occasion throughout the whole drama in which the security forces failed to carry out an order from the established authority, the detention order was not enforced by the police, and Gabheni remained at large. Subsequently, however, he was suspended from his post as Home Affairs Minister, and later dismissed from the *Liqoqo*.

In the interim, the *Liqoqo* had nominated as the new Queen Regent Princess Ntombi – the mother of the already designated heir, the 16-year-old Prince Makhosetive, currently at school in England. In terms of Swazi custom, Ntombi should not have taken over as Queen Mother until the end of the full three-year period of mourning for her late husband. In fact Ntombi initially refused to accept this appointment, firstly on the grounds that she was still in mourning, and secondly, until Dzeliwe voluntarily handed over to her the traditional symbols of royal office. However, Ntombi was eventually prevailed upon to serve as Queen Regent on the terms previously rejected by Dzeliwe. New 'traditional' symbols of office were rapidly invented for her, as Dzeliwe refused to surrender the legitimate symbols. In mid-September, in a further violation of Swazi custom, Makhosetive was flown back to Swaziland and publicly presented as Heir Apparent – a full five years

59

before the prescribed time. This was clearly an attempt to legitimize the usurpation of Dzeliwe. The *Liqoqo* declared that 'ambitious Princes' contesting the confirmation of the new Queen Regent would be regarded as contenders 'having pretensions to the crown of Swaziland', or in other words, guilty of treason against the crown.

A new feature of this phase of struggle for power was that the intense conflicts within the ruling circles finally drew into the political arena forces outside the narrow governing royalist alliance. In the second half of August 1983, the Swazi National Union of Students (SNUS) organized two fairly large demonstrations calling for the reinstatement of both Dzeliwe and Mabandla. They also demanded the abolition of the *Liqoqo*. During this period students approached certain chiefs and Princes, including Gabheni, urging them to lead these demonstrations, or at least openly support them. These requests were declined. Student contacts were also established with the former leadersip of the banned Swaziland National Union of Teachers (SNUT). The second student demonstration of 29 August now included students of the Mbabane Health Science Institute – an expansion of participation which considerably alarmed the authorities. These higher education students clearly expected that school pupils would support their demonstrations. However, at this crucial stage Swaziland schools were on vacation and were only due to reopen on 13 September. Fearing that they would be isolated and that the university itself might be closed, the students' union was eventually prevailed upon to delay any further demonstration at least until the reopening of the schools.

The two weeks between the end of August and the reopening of the schools saw intense manoeuvring by the authorities, to forestall what they feared might be a repeat of the generalized unrest in Swazi educational institutions which had occurred in 1977. Rumours were put around of a compromise which would restore Dzeliwe, at the same time revoking her dismissal of the *Liqoqo*. The threat of student action was finally contained when Bekhimpi informed the former SNUT leadership that the teachers' union would be unbanned if it changed its name to the Swaziland National Association of Teachers, and that it would now be held responsible for any disturbances.

Over the crucial weekend 11–12 September, Prime Minister Bekhimpi made a rapid visit to Mozambique where he met with President Machel. The purpose of this visit was never disclosed. However, there has been widespread speculation in Swaziland that Bekhimpi met with Swazi exiles. In a later public meeting the Prime Minister also claimed that he had received an assurance from President Machel that Mozambique would not allow 'armed bandits' to operate from its territory against Swaziland.[58]

When the schools reconvened on 13 September there were no further demonstrations. This apparent calm gave the *Tibiyo* faction the confidence to have Dzeliwe removed from her kraal and placed under effective house arrest in the Zombodze royal village over the weekend of 17–18 September. During this weekend Ntombi was finally prevailed upon to act as Queen Regent. The following week Makhosetive was presented to the nation.

If the immediate impact of these manoeuvres was to damp down student protest, the long-term effect appears more contradictory. At the height of the crisis an un-named pro-Dzeliwe prince held urgent negotiations with some student leaders, calling on them to take to the streets again in support of Dzeliwe. The students now refused to become involved in what they described as a factional struggle within the Dlamini clan, and declared that they were only prepared to support the Princes in a struggle to abolish the monarchy itself.

The student action apart, there were reports of leaflets being issued in the rural areas, calling on the population to boycott *Tinkundla* meetings to be held in preparation for the 'elections'. Attendance at such meetings was indeed initially poor. Nevertheless, preparations for the elections went ahead. The Authorized Person was given powers to dismiss civil servants, and a purge of the civil service was widely expected following the elections.

d) The October 1983 Elections–August 1984

The final political neutralization of Dzeliwe and her supporters opened the way for the *Tibiyo* faction to take total control over all the apparatuses of the Swazi state. For the moment Queen Ntombi was a pure figurehead, with the Authorized Person, Prince Sozisa, as the effective Regent. The *Tibiyo* faction had long dominated the *Liqoqo*. Now it sought to remove all opposition within this 'supreme council of state' by expelling Prince Gabheni and installing other presumably pliant members. The dismissal of Mabandla had enabled this faction to emerge as dominant in the Cabinet. Through the 'elections' of October 1983 it established its unchallenged hold over both parliament and the Cabinet.

However, this consolidation of complete control over the apparatuses of the Swazi state by the *Tibiyo* faction did not end the struggles for power within the ruling clique. The forces which had coalesced to eliminate first Mabandla and then Dzeliwe and her allies, now turned on each other in a struggle for personal position. This began after the October elections.

Reports on the turn-out at the *Tinkundla* for the 'elections' to the electoral college differ. While the South African liberal newspaper *The Rand Daily Mail* reported a 'massive stay-away',[59] a relatively high level of participation does seem to have occurred, despite calls for a boycott. After a month's deliberations over the list of parliamentary candidates supplied to it by the *Liqoqo*, the electoral college announced the new Swazi parliament at the end of November, with Prime Minister Bekhimpi receiving the most votes. This parliament is unique in Swaziland's post-independence history in that not one direct son of King Sobhuza was 'elected' to it (although two were subsequently appointed by the Queen Regent). As expected, all real and suspected opponents of the now dominant group have been eliminated from both parliament and Cabinet. The only two members of the old Cabinet to appear in the new one are Prime Minister Bekhimpi and Foreign Minister R. V. Dlamini, while the former Deputy Minister of Education, Dabulumjiva Mhlabatsi was appointed Minister in the same department.[60] Significantly, the Managing Director of *Tibiyo*, and one of the most influential figures in this faction, Sishayi Nxumalo, became Finance Minister. Two days later *Tibiyo* was officially designated a 'national development agency' by his ministry, although this has not been ratified by the full Cabinet. Nxumalo was soon replaced as *Tibiyo* Managing Director by former Justice Minister Polycarp Dlamini, though Nxumalo retained his position as Secretary of *Tibiyo*.

To complete their control over all state apparatuses, the ruling clique has initiated its threatened purge of 'disloyal' civil servants, including senior police commanders. Four days after the new Cabinet assumed office, Finance Minister Nxumalo promised to expose the 'rats' in the civil service whom he accused of being responsible for the deficit in state finances.[61] Four senior police commanders were dismissed from their posts, as well as the chairman of the body which coordinates the *Tinkundla* (the latter was, however, later reinstated).

This seizure of total control over all political institutions was matched by a marked increase in repression. An extremely tough anti-sedition law was introduced at the end of 1983 and a number of people charged under it – including the wife of Prince Gabheni. Charges of high treason were brought against 11 prominent Swazis, including one son and two daughters of the late King Sobhuza as well as a leading chief. It was alleged that between September and November 1983 they conspired to depose Queen Regent Ntombi and arrest the Prime Minister and senior members of the security forces.[62] Others were simply detained. Police road blocks are now common in Swaziland. A new system of two-year obligatory National Service (not military service) has been announced. This seeks to instil discipline and respect for tradition amongst the youth. The legal trade unions, small and tightly controlled, have been warned not to meddle in politics.

These repressive measures, designed to consolidate the position of the *Tibiyo* faction, transformed Swaziland into a police state. For the three months following the elections, its leaders seemed to be infused with a siege mentality. Their rhetoric was violent – filled with promises to 'club to death', 'kill' or 'deal with' any opposition. In his Christmas message, Bekhimpi announced a policy of 'an eye for an eye' against those opposing the regime.[63] The chiefs were whipped into line. Shortly before the elections, a *Libandla* meeting was told bluntly by Prince Sozisa – at that time wearing a pistol strapped around his waist – that every chief would have to declare publicly whether he supported Dzeliwe or the new Regent. Those who 'took a certain line' would have to be aware that there would be 'consequences'.[64] In a speech to the nation, Bekhimpi warned 'the children' (i.e. the Swazi people) to leave everything to the elders, who knew what they were doing, and did not have to explain themselves to 'the children'. This was the 'traditional' way of things, he argued.[65]

Events in the southern African region also had a direct and dramatic influence on the pattern of Swazi politics early in 1984. Shortly after the signing of the Nkomati Accord between South Africa and Mozambique, a major crackdown on ANC members in Swaziland began. Though action against the ANC in Swaziland had been taken on a number of occasions since the signing of the then secret non-aggression pact with Pretoria in February 1982, the post-Nkomati offensive against ANC members has been far more intense and has involved an unprecedented level of violence. To some extent this campaign has reflected the hysteria of the domestic crackdown. There have been reports of torture of detained ANC members, of joint interrogations by members of the Swazi and South African police, and even of four ANC cadres being handed over to the apartheid regime.[66] Following a shootout between an ANC group and Swazi police in which a policeman was killed, a major campaign was instituted to mobilize the population against 'foreign armed bandits'.

By the beginning of 1984 all opposition to this new regime appeared for the moment to have been intimidated into quiescence. Under these conditions, signs of a fierce struggle for personal position within the now triumphant *Tibiyo* faction began to emerge. The two contenders for leadership of the faction were Prince Mfanasibili and Dr Sishayi Nxumalo. Each sought at the least to become the undisputed 'power behind the throne', although there are some indications that both men had ambitions for the Prime Ministership.[67] In this struggle for power Mfanasibili's main advantage lay in his position as acknowledged leader of the lineage from which the heir to the throne had been drawn, and hence his influence within the Council of Elders and *Liqoqo*. Nxumalo's main power base, on the other hand, derived from his position as founder and Managing Director of *Tibiyo*.

From the details which have now emerged[68] it appears that the first major move in the power struggle was the dismissal of Nxumalo from his position as Managing Director of *Tibiyo* some weeks after his appointment as Finance Minister. This step which was taken by the *Liqoqo* (and more precisely by the Mfanasibili clique within the *Liqoqo*) struck directly at Nxumalo's power base.

At first Nxumalo responded defensively. Using the position which he still retained as Secretary of *Tibiyo*, he initiated a number of manoeuvres designed to shore up his base in the Fund. According to the *Liqoqo*'s official version of events,[69] after his dismissal Nxumalo first attempted to abolish the post of Managing Director of *Tibiyo* and then to block the appointment of the former Justice Minister, Polycarp Dlamini, to the job. He then arranged for the dismissal of the then General Manager of *Tibiyo*, Sipho Dlamini, and attempted to have appointed instead Prince Dumisa Dlamini (who had been a trade union organizer and member of the Ngwane National Liberatory Congress during the 1960s but for some years had been close to Nxumalo).

In these and later manoeuvres it appears that Nxumalo and his supporters had some success in manipulating the Authorized Person, Prince Sozisa. The importance of Prince Sozisa in these struggles derived from the fact that on assuming office Queen Regent Ntombi had ceded many important powers to sign official state documents to the Authorized Person. This was demanded of her by the *Tibiyo* faction in order to avoid a repetition of the situation in which Dzeliwe had used the

65

discretionary powers then possessed by the Queen Regent to frustrate the *Liqoqo*. Again according to the official *Liqoqo* version of events, Nxumalo supporters convinced the Authorized Person that 'the *Liqoqo* was bewitching him' and that certain of its members wanted to kill him.[70] It does seem clear that at various times the Authorized Person signed issues of the *Government Gazette* dismissing Polycarp Dlamini and reinstating Nxumalo as *Tibiyo* Managing Director, as well as dismissing members of the *Liqoqo* and possibly Prime Minister Prince Bekhimpi. These issues of the *Gazette* were, however, deemed to be invalid by the *Liqoqo* and Regent and never published. The Authorized Person subsequently had his power to sign state documents withdrawn. Some press reports suggested that Prince Sozisa was placed under heavy guard, although he has subsequently been seen at a number of public functions.[71]

This remained more or less the situation until two corruption scandals gave Nxumalo the opportunity to launch a counter-offensive against Mfanasibili and his associates. The first of these broke in March 1984 when the large French-owned fertilizer company, Swaziland Chemical Industries (SCI), was declared bankrupt with debts of R29 million to the Barclays and Standard Banks. In 1982, the exports of SCI had amounted to R55 million, and this single factory was Swaziland's second biggest foreign exchange earner in that year. The apparent clear involvement of associates of Mfanasibili (and in particular *Liqoqo* member Dr George Msibi) in putting pressure on the banks to grant these loans to SCI, enabled Nxumalo to attack Mfanasibili indirectly under the guise of being a concerned public servant merely doing his duty. (In fact Nxumalo has himself been publicly accused of implication in corrupt deals over several years.)[72] At the beginning of March the Minister made a speech in which he charged 'high political figures' with responsibility for the crash of SCI. In the same speech Nxumalo referred to a mysterious incident at the beginning of 1984, when his car rolled a number of times after hitting logs strewn across an isolated road along which he was driving alone.[73] Although he was unhurt, there was speculation that this accident was caused deliberately. At about the same time, Mfanasibili publicly claimed that a 'Gang of Four' – including a Prince and a Cabinet Minister – were plotting a coup.[74] Shortly after, Prince Dumisa, Nxumalo's nominee as General Manager of *Tibiyo*, was sent into exile.

The struggle between the two reached its climax in early June 1984, when the second corruption scandal erupted. This scandal, potentially more serious than the first, involved the fraudulent use of a Swazi-registered company – Liberty Investments – to avoid customs duties. Cars and textiles were imported into Durban supposedly destined for a bonded warehouse in Swaziland. It is alleged that these were in fact sold in South Africa without payment of customs duties. Customs revenue amounting to R13 million is said to have been lost through this fraud. Once again Nxumalo accused 'certain members of the *Liqoqo* who are shareholders' of involvement, and threatened to name them in parliament on Monday 11 June. It later emerged that the chairman of Liberty Investments (a lawyer and businessman by the name of Yussuf Patel) was a close associate of Mfanasibili, and that both Mfanasibili and Msibi had shares in the company.

In the event, Nxumalo was dismissed on Friday 8 June, along with the Minister of Foreign Affairs, R. V. Dlamini, and the army and police chiefs. In its official statement issued four days later, the *Liqoqo* argued that Nxumalo had not acted out of a selfless sense of public duty, but was using these scandals in a bid for personal power. The statement did not deny that corruption had occurred or that senior political figures were involved. Indeed under South African pressure the Swazi government has subsequently been forced to initiate an enquiry into the allegations.

The *Liqoqo* statement further alleged that Nxumalo had led a delegation to Queen Regent Ntombi to demand the restoration of signing powers to the Authorized Person. This, it said, amounted to an attempt to 'illegally remove executive authority from the head and state' and thus constituted 'treason'. Moreover, it claimed that on the day of the dismissal of the four the Queen Regent had been presented with a document for signature dismissing Mfanasibili and George Msibi from the *Liqoqo* on the grounds that 'they had charges to answer'. She had allegedly been told to sign the document or 'face a bloody revolution'. Finally, several attempts were said to have been made to place the security forces on alert without the authority of the *Liqoqo* but with the apparent connivance of the army and police commanders.[75]

Nxumalo, for his part, not surprisingly denied that he had tried to seize power and claimed his dismissal was a straightforward attempt to block his efforts to expose corruption in high places. He further suggested that the reason why the army and police commanders had been dismissed was because they 'refused to arrest him and cover up the corruption'.[76] Although none of the dismissed officials was arrested, Nxumalo had his passport withdrawn on the grounds that he would be called as a material witness in the official investigation of the corruption allegations.

In terms of major policy directions, whether domestic or regional, the impact of the apparent triumph of Mfanasibili over Nxumalo and his associates is likely to be slight. Whereas there were some discernible if limited policy differences between Mabandla and Dzeliwe on the one hand and the *Tibiyo* faction on the other, Nxumalo and Mfanasibili had a broadly common position on most major policy questions. Theirs was a struggle for personal position rather than over the direction state policy should take.

Nevertheless, the dismissal of Nxumalo can be expected to have some impact on the increasingly volatile political situation in Swaziland. Although all opposition appears for the moment to have been intimidated into quiescence, the very manoeuvres by which the *Tibiyo* faction established its dominance, its cynical elimination of Sobhuza's appointed political heirs and immediate family from political life, the blatantly self-serving nature of its rule, and the unpopular, openly collaborationist stance towards South Africa, have clearly had the effect of calling into question the legitimacy of the very institutions of royalist power which this group has always claimed to buttress and defend. The dismissal of the country's Finance Minister just at the moment when, regardless of his own motives and personal reputation, he threatened to reveal details of the involvement in two frauds of the now apparently undisputed 'strong man' of the kingdom, cannot but have diluted further the capacity of the monarchy to continue to function as the ideological cement holding together the contradiction-ridden Swazi kingdom. Moreover, the fact that the Liberty Investment fraud has international dimensions has forced the Swazi government to launch an investigation. Should the powerful South African pressure lead this investigation to conclude that Mfanasibili or his associates were indeed involved, the political instability in the kingdom can only be expected to increase. Finally, the state of morale within the armed forces and police, following the dismissal of their chiefs only a short time after the removal of four other top commanders, must be regarded as somewhat problematical.

The removal of the Ministers appears, moreover, to have some implications for Swazi-South African relations. At the most immediate level the Liberty Investment fraud affects the Southern African Customs Union (SACU) as a whole and not just Swaziland. Nxumalo's dismissal led to a swift South African response. The South African Foreign Minister, Pik Botha, sent a message from Europe to all SACU members countries threatening a South African withdrawal from the agreement if the fraud allegations were not investigated.[77] Although a statement made by Foreign Minister Botha after a visit to Swaziland in July appeared to indicate that Pretoria would not make any direct attempt to reverse the dismissal of Nxumalo and his associates, the force of the South African reaction appears to have persuaded the dominant clique to act with a degree of circumspection with regard to Nxumalo. He remains at liberty within the kingdom and continues to launch attacks on Mfanasibili and his associates through the columns of the South African press.[78] In July he even announced that he would sue Msibi for libel for accusing him of high treason in the official *Liqoqo* statement on his dismissal.[79] For all these reasons it is clear that although

69

Nxumalo is for the moment without any official office in the kingdom, he is far from eliminated as a force in Swazi politics.

6. Swaziland in the Regional Struggle

There are currently two interrelated struggles being waged in the southern African region. The first is the national liberation struggle in South Africa and in Namibia, led by the ANC and SWAPO. The second is the attempt by the nine SADCC states to reduce their economic dependence on South Africa.

Swaziland's position in these struggles is influenced by a number of factors. First and foremost are the deep and increasing links between the governing clique and South African-based monopoly capital. The second is the extremely conservative political and ideological character of the Swazi regime, giving rise, thirdly, to real and definite fears of the possible impact of the advancing liberation struggle on the Swazi population. Finally, the general political climate in the region, and more particularly the actions of the SADCC countries and Frontline states, also have a certain impact on the regional stance of the Swazi regime.

The interplay between these factors is complex and leads to numerous small shifts and turns in Swaziland's position. Nevertheless, in general, the balance between them has led to the emergence and maintenance throughout the post-independence period of a fundamentally conservative foreign and regional policy – one which cannot simply be conceived of as an inevitable consequence of the geographic and economic position of Swaziland. The Swazi regime has thus consistently refused to render any concrete support to the liberation movements of the region (and more particularly the ANC, or, before 1974, Frelimo). Indeed it has taken various active steps to prevent such movements operating on its territory.[80] Moreover, no serious effort has been made to seek alternatives to links with South Africa; on the contrary, since independence these have deepened and continue to do so. In the period prior to Mozambican independence, Swaziland also maintained close and even cordial relations with the Portuguese colonial regime.

Whilst these factors all tend to push Swazi regional policy in a conservative direction, there are nevertheless countervailing influences. Thus, firstly, whilst 95% of Swazi imports come from South Africa, most of the country's exports are sent outside the southern African region. Furthermore, Swaziland has received considerable aid from international bodies – particularly United Nations agencies, and more recently, potentially through SADCC. Continued access to such aid, as well as concessions in respect of export prices through Commonwealth agencies and the Lomé Convention, depend to some extent at least on the Swazi regime not being seen to be the mere puppet of Pretoria.

Moreover, post-independence expectations that membership of the Southern African Customs Union (SACU) would create possibilities for the emergence of Swazi-based industries producing for the South African market have by and large not been realized. This is partly because of blocking action by South African capital, and the state seeking to prevent competition from industrial production in the BLS countries. This has generated some anger in influential circles. The Managing Director of the state-owned National Industrial Corporation of Swaziland has in fact publicly stated that the country's membership of SACU is a major hindrance to its attempts to industrialize.[81] It has also given rise to limited attempts to seek other markets in the region.

The Swazi regime further appears aware of the inevitable domestic political risks of being seen by its own population to be closly identified with the apartheid regime. At the regional level, the actions of the SADCC countries and Frontline states have had some restraining impact on the Swazi regime's stance in the region. Finally, there have been intangible ideological factors whose effect is difficult either to assess or predict. The most important here was the express reluctance of King Sobhuza to act openly against the ANC, for the apparent reason that the Swazi monarchy was involved in its formation in 1912 and retained some sentimental attachment to the organization.

Taken together, all of these factors have acted with variable effects in different periods as a restraining force against the emergence of open collaboration with the apartheid regime in the region. This was particularly true in the early post-independence years. In the late 1960s and early 1970s, the Swazi regime was noticeably less co-operative with Pretoria on a number of issues than, for instance, the Jonathan regime in Lesotho – which was then the apartheid regime's most pliable regional ally. In 1969 Swaziland endorsed the Lusaka Manifesto declaring that African states would only enter into dialogue with Pretoria to discuss the mechanisms of the transfer of power in South Africa. In 1970, Swaziland (along with Lesotho, the Ivory Coast and four other states) abstained rather than opposed an OAU resolution condemning the 'dialogue offensive' that the Vorster regime was then mounting. It also opposed South Africa's position on Namibia in numerous UN resolutions and accepted South African refugees (including ANC members), albeit with certain limitations.

However, Swaziland has been markedly affected by the intensified regional and internal South African struggle since the mid-1970s. The Swazi ruling class has come under increased pressure from the contending forces in these struggles. The apartheid regime has demanded that Swaziland impose further restrictions on refugees, and act with greater vigour against any real or imagined attempts by ANC guerrillas to traverse Swazi territory. The objective of getting neighbouring states to act as police agents for the apartheid regime is well summarized by the prominent Afrikaner nationalist academic with close links to the Pretoria regime, Deon Geldenhuys:

> Neighbouring states [must not be] used as springboards for guerrilla or terrorist attacks on South Africa. South Africa clearly not only wants neighbouring governments to give an undertaking to this effect, but also wants them to apply it effectively, thus ensuring that 'unauthorized' incursions do not take place. Furthermore, South Africa would wish that black states in the region . . . would not allow the fighters transit facilities or allow the movements to open offices in their countries.[82]

As part of its policy to extend its potential leverage over neighbouring states the apartheid regime has also sought to deepen economic links with Swaziland and forge a firmer political alliance.

To these ends Pretoria has deployed a variety of measures. In 1978 and 1979 South Africa offered Swaziland, together with other states in the region, the prospect of 'co-operating' with them in a range of infrastructural projects through the institutions of the proposed Constellation of Southern African States (CONSAS). When the states of the region, including Swaziland, refused to associate with the CONSAS project, and as the armed struggle in South Africa intensified, threats were made to turn Swaziland into a 'second front'. This was backed up by a number of incursions, in 1980 and early 1981, by agents of the apartheid regime operating against refugee targets. Later in 1981, Swaziland was offered a number of specific 'incentives' if it would 'co-operate with Pretoria', particularly on the question of South Africa's demands concerning ANC refugees. These incentives included support for the construction of a railway link connecting the Komatipoort region of South Africa with the Richards Bay port, via Swaziland. It is calculated that this project will make the Swazi railways profitable for the first time. More important, Swaziland was offered the cession of South African territory – the KaNgwane bantustan and the Ngwavuma area of the KwaZulu bantustan – in the notorious 'land deal'. Finally, in 1982 and 1983 the distribution of revenue under the customs union agreement, and the prospect of a payment by South Africa of a 'premium' to its 'friends' – R50 million to Swaziland in 1982 – was a further enticement dangled before the Swazi government.

As was revealed in March 1984, the Swazi regime had succumbed to these pressures by early 1982. In February 1982 it signed a secret non-aggression pact with Pretoria. The terms of this agreement commit both states to 'combat terrorism, insurgency and subversion individually and collectively' and to 'call upon each other wherever possible for such assistance and steps as may be deemed necessary'.[83] As long as Swaziland was unique among southern African states in taking such a step, it remained to some extent susceptible to countervailing pressures from the Frontline states and the OAU. Thus although a number of actions were taken against ANC members in the kingdom, by current standards these remained relatively mild. However, with the signing of the Nkomati Accord between Mozambique and South Africa, Swaziland has embraced its relationship with the apartheid regime with a renewed vigour and frankness. South African Defence Force personnel in uniform and carrying arms were openly welcomed into Swaziland to provide 'technical aid' in the rebuilding of roads and bridges damaged by cyclone Domoina. In May 1984 the Prime Minister led a large delegation on an official visit to South Africa, where the cordial relations and close co-operation between the countries in a number of areas, including security, were strssed. It was later announced that the two states would establish formal diplomatic relations, probably at Trade Commissioner level. Finally, within Swaziland itself, the hostility expressed against the ANC by senior government officials has reached a level of near hysteria.

Even before the most recent developments, one commentator described Swaziland as South Africa's most faithful ally and closest collaborator in the region.[84] This is now more true than ever.

Notes

1. See P. Bonner, *Kings, Commoners and Concessionaries* (Cambridge University Press, Cambridge, 1983).
2. J. Daniel, 'The Political Economy of Colonial and Post-Colonial Swaziland', *South African Labour Bulletin*, Vol. 7, No. 6, 1982, p. 93. The main street of Swziland's capital, Mbabane, remains named after this arch-colonialist.
3. The term *induna* means an administrator/councillor appointed by the King. It could be applied to Ministers as well. In this specific case, however, such appointed *indunas* were clearly seen as overseers.
4. See M. Fransman, 'The State and Development in Swaziland 1960–1977', D.Phil. thesis, University of Sussex, 1978.
5. This company has extensive fruit farm interests in South Africa, particularly in the KwaZulu bantustan. It seems that the company intends to can the bulk of its produce at the Swaziland factory, and so gain admission to the EEC market for such 'products of Swaziland' in terms of the Lomé Convention.
6. The Kirsch group is still controlled by its chairman, Natie Kirsch, although South Africa's second biggest non-state monopoly, SANLAM, has recently acquired a 49.9% share of the new holding company – Sanki – which now controls all of the Kirsch group's interests. Kirsch himself is a white Swazi citizen. In the early 1960s he was a settler maize farmer in Swaziland and leader of the so-called Committee of 12 which rallied settler support for the King's INM party. Kirsch managed to secure control of the maize milling and traditional beer brewing market in Swaziland, which provided the base for his fortune. In the early 1970s he moved into South Africa. The Kirsch group is now a giant conglomerate with assets in South Africa alone of close to R2,000 million in 1982, and interets in many sectors of the South African economy. The group also has substantial investments in the USA. Today its Swazi operations provide less than 1% of the annual turnover of the South African-based group. Natie Kirsch himself, however, retains considerable influence in Swazi politics.
7. See S. Ettinger, 'The Economics of the Customs Union Between Botswana, Lesotho, Swaziland and South Africa', Ph.D. dissertation, University of Michigan, 1974.

8. Daniel, 'The Political Economy of Colonial and Post-Colonial Swaziland', p. 108.
9. See p. 41 for a discussion of the composition of the monarchy and chieftancy and of the institutional linkages which sustain them.
10. All figures cited here for *Tibiyo* are drawn from *Tibiyo Taka Ngwane*, 'Balance Sheet and Notes to the Financial Statement for the year ended 30 April 1981.
11. Shortly after his appointment as Minister of Finance following the October 1983 elections, Nxumalo was replaced by former Justice Minister Polycarp Dlamini as Managing Director of *Tibiyo*. However, he remains Secretary of the Fund.
12. 'Swaziland Economy in 1981 and Forecast for 1982', US Embassy, Swaziland, 17 May 1982.
13. Central Statistical Office, *Annual Statistical Bulletin, 1980* (hereafter *ASB 80*) (Mbabane), Table G.3, p. 37.
14. See note 6 above.
15. Central Statistical Office, *Employment and Wages, 1981* (hereafter *EW 81*) (Mbabane), Table 2, p. 5, and Table 12, p. 11.
16. *EW 81*, Tables 3, 6, 7 and 12. These figures should be treated with some caution, as official statistics often do not tally. Thus, while the source cited in Table 2 puts the number of manufacturing establishments in 1978/9 at 57, the source cited here gives the number as 81 in 1978 and 76 in 1979, whilst the total numbers in paid employment for these years are given as 8.743 and 8.938 respectively (compared with the 12.655 cited in Table 2 for 1978/9).
17. *EW 81*, Table A4, p. 32. Again, discrepancies in the same statistical source exist. Thus the table cited here gives the total number of private construction establishments as 33, while table A1 on p. 29 of the same source puts the figure at 41. Both tables list the same total numbers employed in private construction.
18. These conceptions and categories are enshrined in official statistics. See e.g. *ASB 80*, p. 21.
19. *ASB 80*, p. 24, and Barclays Bank, *Swaziland: An Economic Survey and Businessman's Guide*, (Mbabane, 1981), Table A, p. 6.
20. Margo Russel, 'The Rural Swazi Homestead in Context', in F. de Vletter et al, *The Rural Swazi Homestead*, (Social Science Research Unit, University of Swaziland, 1983), p. 321.

21. Cited in F. de Vletter, 'A Socio-economic Profile of the Rural Swazi Homestead', ibid., p. 27.
22. Ibid.
23. F. de Vletter, 'Labour Migration in Swaziland', *South African Labour Bulletin*, Vol. 7, No. 6, 1982, p. 121.
24. Ibid., pp. 119–120.
25. Ibid., and *EW 81*, Table 5, p. 7.
26. *ASB 80*, Table F.4, p. 23.
27. *EW 80*, Table A.1, p. 29. A further 5,143 were employed in forestry to give a total for the industrial census category 'agriculture and forestry' of 24,055. Again, this does not tally with the total given in Table 2, p. 5 of the same source.
28. Ibid., Table 4, p. 6.
29. Ibid., Table A.5, p. 32.
30. Patricia McFadden, 'Women in Wage-Labour in Swaziland: A Focus on Agriculture', *South African Labour Bulletin*, Vol. 7, No. 6, p. 148 et passim.
31. *EW 81*, Table 2, p. 5.
32. Ibid., Table A.1, p. 29 and Table 20, p. 16.
33. 'Budget Speech' in *Weekend Observer* (of Swaziland) 25 February 1984.
34. Ibid., and 'Economic Review', Prime Minister's Office (Mbabane, 1983).
35. See *Sunday Tribune*, 4 March 1984.
36. *Weekend Observer*, 25 February 1984.
37. Ibid., and 'Economic Review', Prime Minister's Office (Mbabane, 1983).
38. Ibid.
39. 'Budget Speech: Kingdom of Swaziland', presented by the Finance Minister, 17 February 1983, mimeo. *Weekend Observer*, 25 February 1984.
40. Barclays Bank, *Swaziland*, p. 28.
41. *Weekend Observer*, 25 February 1984.
42. *ASB 80*, Table A, p. 1, and Table C.5, p. 11.
43. See note 23.
44. For a theoretical discussion of this issue, see M. Legassick & H. Wolpe, 'The Bantustans and Capital Accumulation in South Africa', *Review of African Political Economy*, 7, 1976.
45. *EW 81*, Table 2, p. 5, Table 18, p. 15, and Table 5, p. 7.
46. *ASB 80*, p. 9.
47. However, see p. 68 for an analysis of why this may now be

breaking down.

48. 'Budget Speech' for 1983, *Weekend Observer*, 25 February 1984.

49. Small dealers are frequently obliged to pay a patronage retainer to members of the royalist circles. One Mbabane shopkeeper is known to pay R2000 each month to a prominent member of the *Liqoqo*.

50. King Sobhuza was named Heir Apparent when he was still a baby, following the death of his father. However, given the particular circumstances of Sobhuza's nomination as future King over one of his father's other sons, Makosekose, the lineage descendants of Makosekose were apparently expected to provide the successor to Sobhuza. Prince Mfanasibili is now accepted as the current head of this lineage until Prince Makhosetive comes of age.

51. The 'electoral' procedure is as follows. On the day announced all adults are supposed to present themselves at their *Tinkundla*. Here they find four candidates, nominated by the monarch, and each standing beside a gate. No speeches nor discussion of political positions takes place. The population then march through the gate of the individuals they prefer. The two individuals with the most 'votes' are thus elected to the electoral college. The electoral college is then presented with a list of parliamentary candidates by the monarch, from among which it chooses 40 MPs. The monarch then appoints a further 10.

52. This section is based on a reading of the Swazi press and more particularly on a series of interviews.

53. In mid 1981 reports began to surface of an 'offer' by South Africa to Swaziland to cede to the latter the KaNgwane bantustan and Ngwavuma section of the KwaZulu bantustan. Mabandla's vocal opposition to the land deal has now been made public in a document published by the *Liqoqo*, entitled 'Mabandla's Litany of Betrayal', *Times of Swaziland*, 10 August 1983. The background and details of the controversial land deal issue are dealt with in South African Research Service/ Development Studies Group, Information Publication No. 7, *The Swaziland-South Africa Land Deal* (Johannesburg, 1982). After encountering fierce resistance to the proposal both on the part of the populations and bantustan authorities in the areas affected, the apartheid regime referred the matter to the Rumpff Commission of Inquiry. In June 1984, however, the Commission

was dissolved, apparently because the Botha regime was unwilling to accept its principal recommendation – that a referendum on the issue be held in the KaNgwane and Ngwavuma regions. The Swazi authorities were subsequently informed that any 'border adustments' would have to be negotiated with the bantustan administrations of the areas concerned. At the tim of writing it is unclear whether this is intended as a means of quietly shelving the issue, or as a manoeuvre by Pretoria to draw an OAU member into according a degree of *de facto* recognition to the bantustans.

54. The *Times of Swaziland* reported a 'marked military atmosphere' with armed troops 'swarming around the royal residence', 21 March 1983. Curiously, the announcement of the Prime Minister's dismissal was made by the Governor of the Lobamba Royal Residence and not by the Authorized Person as it should constitutionally have been.

55. *Times of Swaziland*, 21 November 1983.

56. Dzeliwe had agreed to Mabandla's dismissal only with great reluctace and on condition that she alone nominated his successor.

57. *Times of Swaziland*, 10 August 1983.

58. *Swazi Observer*, 10 October 1983.

59. *Swazi Observer*, 29 October 1983.

60. Earlier expectations that Mfanasibili would replace Bekhimpi were not realized. Shortly before the elections Mfanasibili began to walk with a marked limp. He claimed it was the result of being bewitched. Whatever the truth of the matter, it is almost universally believed in Swaziland that Mfanasibili was shot in the leg, and the Princes with him shot dead, by an army guard, when they tried to enter King Sobhuza's tomb with the apparent intention of removing the bones. The soldier who is supposed to have shot Mfanasibili was himself detained and later died in detention. No explanation for his death has been forthcoming. See *Drum*, December 1983.

61. *Swazi Observer*, 26 November 1983.

62. *Times of Swaziland*, 9 December 1983.

63. See *Swazi News*, 24 December 1983.

64. *Times of Swaziland*, 10 October 1983.

65. *Swazi Observer*, 31 August 1983.

66. See *City Press*, 20 May 1984.

67. See note 61 above on the generally accepted reasons for the

failure of Mfanasibili's bid to secure the Premiership after the October 1983 elections.

68. Reprinted in *Swazi Observer*, 12 June 1984.
69. Ibid.
70. Ibid.
71. *Drum*, May 1984.
72. In July 1984 it was announced that the Ombudsman had initiated investigations into Nxumalo's alleged involvement whilst Managing Director of *Tibiyo*, in a R809,000 fraud (see *Swazi Observer*, 13 July 1984). This investigation appears to be an act of revenge by the now dominant clique within the *Liqoqo*.
73. *Sunday Tribune*, 4 March 1984.
74. *The Citizen*, 3 April 1984.
75. *Swazi Observer*, 12 June 1984.
76. See *Times of Swaziland*, 11 June 1984.
77. *Sunday Times*, 10 June 1984.
78. See, for example, interview given to *Sunday Express*, 17 July 1984.
79. *Times of Swaziland*, 4 July 1984.
80. In 1968 the regime declared that if guerrilla fighters traversed Swazi territory on their way to South Africa, it would call for support from the apartheid regime. This was later modified to a declaration that the Swazi armed forces would carry out the task themselves.
81. Interview, March 1983.
82. 'Some Strategic Implications of Regional Economic Relationships for the Republic of South Africa', *Strategic Review* (Institute for Strategic Studies, University of Pretoria, January 1981).
83. *The Citizen*, 2 April 1984.
84. Anon., 'Swaziland: South Africa's willing captive', *Work in Progress*, 27, 1983.

Appendix

The Swazi Cabinet as announced by the Prime Minister, 21 November 1983

Prime Minister   Prince Bekhimpi Dlamini

Ministers:

Finance	Dr Sishayi Nxumalo (dismissed 8 June 1984)
Justice	David Matse
Health	Prince Phiwokwakhe Dlamini
Education	Dabulumjiva Mhlabatsi
Foreign Affairs	Richard Velaphi Dlamini (dismissed 8 June 1984)
Labour & Public Service	Mhlangano Matsebulo
Defence & Youth	Col. Fonono Dube
Agriculture & Cooperatives	Sipho Hezekeil Mamba
Commerce, Industry, Mines & Economic Planning	Derik von Wissel
Natural Resources & Land Utilization and Energy	Prince Khuzulwandle Dlamini
Interior & Immigration	King Mtetwa
Works & Communications	Chief Sipho Shongwe
Without Portfolio	Mhambi Mnisi

AFRICA TITLES FROM ZED

Dan Nabudere
IMPERIALISM IN EAST AFRICA
Vol. I: Imperialism and Exploitation
Vol. II: Imperialism and Integration
Hb

Elenga M'Buyinga
PAN AFRICANISM OR NEO
COLONIALISM?
The Bankruptcy of the OAU
Hb and Pb

Bade Onimode
IMPERIALISM AND
UNDERDEVELOPMENT IN
NIGERIA
The Dialectics of Mass Poverty
Hb and Pb

Michael Wolfers and Jane Bergerol
ANGOLA IN THE FRONTLINE
Hb and Pb

Mohamed Babu
AFRICAN SOCIALISM OR
SOCIALIST AFRICA?
Hb and Pb

Anonymous
INDEPENDENT KENYA
Hb and Pb

Yolamu Barongo (Editor)
POLITICAL SCIENCE IN AFRICA:
A RADICAL CRITIQUE
Hb and Pb

Okwudiba Nnoli (Editor)
PATH TO NIGERIAN
DEVELOPMENT
Pb

Emile Vercruijsse
THE PENETRATION OF
CAPITALISM
A West African Case Study
Hb

Fatima Babikir Mahmoud
THE SUDANESE BOURGEOISIE
— Vanguard of Development?
Hb and Pb

No Sizwe
ONE AZANIA, ONE NATION
The National Question in South
Africa
Hb and Pb

Ben Turok (Editor)
DEVELOPMENT IN ZAMBIA
A Reader
Pb

J. F Rweyemamu (Editor)
INDUSTRIALIZATION AND
INCOME DISTRIBUTION IN
AFRICA
Hb and Pb

Claude Ake
REVOLUTIONARY PRESSURES
IN AFRICA
Hb and Pb

Anne Seidman and Neva Makgetla
OUTPOSTS OF MONOPOLY
CAPITALISM
Southern Africa in the Changing
Global Economy
Hb and Pb

Peter Rigby
PERSISTENT PASTORALISTS
Nomadic Societies in Transition
Hb and Pb

Edwin Madunagu
PROBLEMS OF SOCIALISM: THE
NIGERIAN CHALLENGE
Pb

Mai Palmberg
THE STRUGGLE FOR AFRICA
Hb and Pb

Chris Searle
WE'RE BUILDING THE NEW SCHOOL!
Diary of a Teacher in Mozambique
Hb (at Pb price)

Cedric Robinson
BLACK MARXISM
The Making of the Black Radical Tradition
Hb and Pb

Eduardo Mondlane
THE STRUGGLE FOR MOZAMBIQUE
Pb

Basil Davidson
NO FIST IS BIG ENOUGH TO HIDE THE SKY
The Liberation of Guinea Bissau and Cape Verde:
Aspects of the African Revolution
Hb and Pb

Baruch Hirson
YEAR OF FIRE, YEAR OF ASH
The Soweto Revolt: Roots of a Revolution?
Hb and Pb

SWAPO Department of Information and Publicity
TO BE BORN A NATION
The Liberation Struggle for Namibia
Pb

Peder Gouwenius
POWER OF THE PEOPLE
South Africa in Struggle: A Pictorial History
Pb

Gillian Walt and Angela Melamed (Editors)
MOZAMBIQUE: TOWARDS A PEOPLE'S HEALTH SERVICE
Pb

Horst Drechsler
LET US DIE FIGHTING
The Struggle of the Herero and Nam Against German Imperialism (1884 1915)
Hb and Pb

Andre Astrow
ZIMBABWE: A REVOLUTION THAT LOST ITS WAY?
Hb and Pb

Rene Lefort
ETHIOPIA: AN HERETICAL REVOLUTION?
Hb and Pb

Robert H. Davies, Dan O'Meara an Sipho Dlamini
THE STRUGGLE FOR SOUTH AFRICA
A Reference Guide to Movements, Organizations and Institutions
Hb and Pb

Joseph Hanlon
MOZAMBIQUE: THE REVOLUTION UNDER FIRE
Hb and Pb

Henry Isaacs
LIBERATION MOVEMENTS IN CRISIS
The PAC of South Africa
Hb and Pb

Toyin Falola and Julius Ihonvbere
THE RISE AND FALL OF NIGERIA'S SECOND REPUBLIC, 1979-83
Hb and Pb

Dianne Bolton
NATIONALIZATION: A ROAD TC SOCIALISM?
The Case of Tanzania
Pb

A.T. Nzula, I.I. Potekhin and A.Z. Zusmanovich
FORCED LABOUR IN COLONIAL AFRICA
Hb and Pb

Jeff Crisp
THE STORY OF AN AFRICAN WORKING CLASS
— Ghanaian Miners' Struggles, 1870-1980
Hb and Pb

Aquino de Braganca and Immanuel Wallerstein (Editors)
THE AFRICAN LIBERATION READER
Documents of the National Liberation Movements
Vol I: The Anatomy of Colonialism
Vol II: The National Liberation Movements
Vol III: The Strategy of Liberation
Hb and Pb

Faarax M.J. Cawl
IGNORANCE IS THE ENEMY OF LOVE
Pb

Kinfe Abraham
FROM RACE TO CLASS
Links and Parallels in African and Black American Protest Expression
Pb

Robert Mshengu Kavanagh
THEATRE AND CULTURAL STRUGGLE IN SOUTH AFRICA
A Study in Cultural Hegemony and Social Conflict
Hb and Pb

A. Temu and B. Swai
HISTORIANS AND AFRICANIST HISTORY: A CRITIQUE
Hb and Pb

Robert Archer and Antoine Bouillon
THE SOUTH AFRICAN GAME
Sport and Racism
Hb and Pb

Ray et al.
DIRTY WORK 2
The CIA in Africa
Pb

Raqiya Haji Dualeh Abdalla
SISTERS IN AFFLICTION
Circumcision and Infibulation of Women in Africa
Hb and Pb

Christine Obbo
AFRICAN WOMEN
Their Struggle for Economic Independence
Pb

Maria Rose Cutrufelli
WOMEN OF AFRICA
Roots of Oppression
Hb and Pb

Asma El Dareer
WOMAN, WHY DO YOU WEEP?
Circumcision and Its Consequences
Hb and Pb

Miranda Davies (Editor)
THIRD WORLD — SECOND SEX
Women's Struggles and National Liberation
Hb and Pb

Organization of Angolan Women
ANGOLAN WOMEN BUILDING THE FUTURE
From National Liberation to Women's Emancipation
Hb and Pb

Zed Books' titles cover Africa, Asia, Latin America and the Middle East, as well as general issues affecting the Third World's relations with the rest of the world. Our Series embrace: Imperialism, Women, Political Economy, History, Labour, Voices of Struggle, Human Rights and other areas pertinent to the Third World.

You can order Zed titles direct from Zed Books Ltd., 57 Caledonian Road, London N1 9BU, UK.